Love
Unleashes
Life

STEPHANIE GRAY

ABORTION
AND THE ART OF
COMMUNICATING TRUTH

Life Cycle Books
Toronto, Ontario • Fort Collins, Colorado

Cover Design by: Matthew Dyck

Published & distributed by Life Cycle Books
www.lifecyclebooks.com   orders@lifecyclebooks.com

Printed in Canada

When names have an asterisk* next to them in this book, that is an indication that the person's real name is not being used.

Library and Archives Canada Cataloguing in Publication

Gray, Stephanie, 1980-, author
     Love unleashes life : abortion & the art of communicating
     truth / by Stephanie Gray.

ISBN 978-0-919225-48-0 (paperback)

1. Pro-life movement. 2. Abortion--Moral and ethical aspects.
I. Title.

HQ767.15.G73 2016   363.46   C2015-908565-9

To Pops and Mom - who taught me how to use
my head and my heart.

Table of Contents

Introduction

Aaron called me out. And so he should have. I *was* being unkind. We were strangers who happened to meet near a pro-life exhibit. We started discussing abortion and I could sense feelings welling up inside me—feelings of judgment, annoyance, and frustration towards him.

And I let those feelings spill over into my interaction— my tone, my sharpness, and my stubbornness, until Aaron finally said, "You're not like the other guy. I talked with John and he was really nice. You're being mean."

I was embarrassed, and I should have been: I *was* being mean. I was wrong. My error lied not in my position on abortion but in *how I was communicating it* to someone who held a different view.

I once heard pro-life speaker Jay Watts say that the pro-life movement needs "good arguments by good arguers."[1] While I certainly had the former, I was failing at the latter. But thanks to Aaron calling me out for it to my face, I apologized to him in that very moment and changed how I interacted with him before we parted ways.

For over a decade it has been my full-time job to have abortion conversations with people who don't share the pro-life view. While it can be tempting to focus more on *what* we are saying, than on *who* we are saying something to, countless interactions have taught me the importance of looking at a conversation as an encounter with another soul. How important it is that we be gentle with people, that we not make assumptions, but instead that we seek to understand. Through trial, error, and success, I offer to you the experiences and insights I've had from this broad range of encounters so that you can communicate truth with grace.

While we certainly need the strongest of minds, we also need the most tender of hearts. That was lacking in my interaction with Aaron, but present in many other encounters. This book will draw on a vast array of experiences and knowledge in order to equip people of faith how to successfully dialogue about abortion with our secular, and wounded, culture.

Chapter 1
Communicating Well

The Power of Questions[2]

If you spend any time with young children you'll notice something pretty quick: they ask a lot of questions. Children are keen to learn and that is evidenced by their favorite question, "Why?"

Asking questions has an effect on the minds that do the asking—but also on the minds that do the answering. It's often only when we're asked to explain something that we realize whether we have answers, and whether those answers make sense.

That was my experience transitioning from high school to university. I went from an environment where the people around me believed as I did, to a place where they didn't—and I was challenged at my core. Friends in dorm would ask me questions about my beliefs and I found myself struggling to articulate good reasons behind my claims.

Looking back, I'm grateful for those questions, because they set me on a journey to seek truth, to nourish my mind, and as a result, improve my life. I discovered that not knowing the "Why?" behind my beliefs was an opportunity to hunt for good explanations. I found them, and it strengthened my convictions.

Questions have power. They can set us on a journey looking for answers we previously didn't know. Or, they can draw out of us answers that, deep down, we *did* know but hadn't acknowledged until the opportunity arose from a question.

Questions Change Us

The latter was the experience of my friend Rachel when she interviewed for a year's missionary program in the United States. The program director asked her, "If you didn't do our program, what would you do?" Rachel didn't skip a beat when answering: "I'd go to Africa."

That question, and her answer, played over and over in Rachel's mind for 24 hours until she had an epiphany: "I need to go to Africa!" And so she did. For Rachel, serving the people in Africa was a deep desire of her heart. But for whatever reason, she had never pursued it until she was asked a question. And answering that question put her on a very different trajectory.

I had a similar experience when reading Matthew Kelly's book *The Rhythm of Life: Living Every Day With Passion and Purpose*. Near the beginning, he asks readers to put the book down and write a list of their dreams. His captivating writing moved me to pull out my journal and think big.

That day, on January 29, 2006, I began to transcribe my dreams. My fifth one was this: "to visit an orphanage and hold and love the children." The question had unleashed a passion, and the answer motivated me to act: Two years later, in May 2008, I travelled to a small village in Romania and cared for needy children.

Rachel and I were changed. Why? Because we were asked— and subsequently answered—questions.

Follow the Example of Jesus

If this tactic of asking questions is so transformational, it shouldn't surprise people of faith that Jesus embraced it too.

In Luke 10:25, Jesus is approached by a lawyer, a scholar of the law, who asks him, "Teacher, what shall I do to inherit eternal life?" And Jesus wisely asks questions: "What is written in the law? How do you read it?"

Instead of getting onto a soap box and pushing information into the lawyer, Jesus asks questions and draws information *out of* the lawyer. In doing so, if the lawyer has any objections, he'll ultimately be arguing with himself.

This was a communication strategy Jesus began well before His thirties. Luke's Gospel recounts the story of 12-year-old Jesus being accidentally left behind by Joseph and Mary in Jerusalem during Passover:

"After three days they found him in the temple, sitting among the teachers, listening to them and asking them questions" (Luke 2:46).

What was Jesus doing? *Listening and asking questions.* And when Jesus employed this strategy, the Scriptures tell us, "all who heard Him were amazed at His understanding and His answers" (Luke 2:47).

Questions lead the questioner to information. Questions lead the answerer to clarity. Questions create an atmosphere of respect where people listen to one another, and that leads to understanding.

Seek to Understand

In 1912, a prayer was published in France in a small spiritual magazine *La Clochette (The Little Bell)*. In time, these words, in their early days, called Prayer for Peace, have been most associated (possibly inaccurately) with Roman Catholic Saint Francis of Assisi, dubbed "The Prayer of St. Francis."[3]

Regardless of whoever coined the prayer, its sentiment is a beautiful expression that should guide any conversation—whether about abortion or anything else:

> Lord make me an instrument of your peace.
> Where there is hatred, let me sow love;
> Where there is injury, pardon;
> Where there is doubt, faith;
> Where there is despair, hope;
> Where there is darkness, light;
> And where there is sadness, joy.
>
> O Divine Master, grant that I may not so much seek
> to be consoled, as to console;
> To be understood, as to understand;
> To be loved, as to love.
> For it is in giving that we receive;
> It is in pardoning that we are pardoned;
> And it is in dying that we are born to eternal life.

O Divine Master, grant that I may not so much seek to be understood as to understand. That's what questions do—they help us to understand.

In order to understand, we need to listen deeply to what the other person says. If people see that we have a strong mind and a soft heart, they'll be more likely to dialogue with us and consider what we have to say. It is imperative that pro-life conviction not override pro-life compassion because it is not so much about simply winning a debate as it is about changing hearts. As we're told in 1 Peter 3:15, "Always be prepared to make a defense to any one who calls you to account for the hope that is in you" which is immediately followed up by, "yet do it with gentleness and reverence."

The Power of Stories

Not only do questions have a particular power, but so do stories. My niece and nephew often say to me, "Auntie Steph! Can you tell us a story from the mouth?" Not realizing that in asking me to make up a story what they're really asking is that I tell a story from my mind, they nonetheless are conveying a love for something instilled in us humans from a young age: storytelling.

Stories are at the heart of so much of our communications—from novels to movies to songs, the human experience drives us to constantly seek out, and tell, stories. Good teachers do this. Good presenters do this. And good parents do this. Why?

Stories have a way of captivating us, of engaging our imagination. Stories have a way of taking settings and characters we can relate to, or understand, and inserting principles—life lessons—into them in a way that is easier to accept than if we were told a principle in isolation. In other words, they connect an important idea to a particular audience.

Again, Jesus illustrates this for us when communicating with the lawyer in Luke 10. After the lawyer acknowledges that the law says we are to love—to love God and to love neighbor—he asks Jesus a question: "Who is my neighbor?" (Luke 10:29) This time, Jesus responds with a story: The Parable of the Good Samaritan.

Jesus' listeners knew how dangerous the road to Jericho was. They knew who Priests and Levites were; they also knew who Samaritans were. They knew it was probable for someone travelling down that road to come under attack. And it is within this setting that Jesus illustrates who one's neighbor is and what love of him looks like—seeking the other's good, meeting the other's needs, self-sacrifice, and not letting legalistic rules or ethnic differences get in the way. But He didn't directly say any of that. He *showed* it through the power of a story.

Throughout this book, questions and stories form the core of communicating the pro-life message, for it is these which lead to fruitful encounters where people are both drawn to the truth and where people experience the respect owed their person. But the *kinds* of questions and stories you use will vary—depending on the life experience and disposition of the person you are speaking with.

There are some for whom ignorance is the challenge—they simply don't know. When they hear a logical pro-life argument, they become enlightened—a reaction of the head. But there are others for whom the problem is denial, and as pro-life leader Gregg Cunningham has pointed out, those in denial *don't want* to know, so that logic is often impenetrable to their minds—theirs is a reaction of the heart. Often a personal experience, or that of a loved one, creates a wall, making a simple appeal to reason not so simple to accept. To ensure we are best equipped to reach all, this book will help you communicate well to both the head and the heart.

Chapter 2

The Disposition of A Good Communicator

Physician and poet William Carlos Williams once said, "It's not what you say that matters but the manner in which you say it."

Before we look at how to apply questions and stories to conversations that reach the head and the heart, it's important we not overlook this fundamental point: our disposition when communicating matters—it really, *really* matters. It makes all the difference in the world.

Whose Power?

The night of Jesus' arrest that would lead to His scourging, crucifixion and resurrection, Scripture tells us, "[H]e... knelt down and prayed" (Luke 22:41). Amidst Jesus' teaching ministry, we're told, "[H]e went up into the hills by himself to pray" (Matthew 14:23), and at another point, "And in the morning, a great while before day, he rose and went out to a lonely place, and there he prayed" (Mark 1:35). Jesus' words and actions were grounded in prayer. Ours should be as well.

When we enter into conversations, a vital question for each of us to consider is this: Have I invited God along? Am I running on human strength or Divine? Have I prayed that I would decrease so that God may increase? Have I taken time for God to work in me before I take time to do His work?

We encounter people for such a brief moment compared to a lifetime, and in some cases we never see them again. This fact should serve to remind us of our littleness in comparison to God's greatness. Further, it should be a sobering reminder to us of our influence to do great good or great evil—as someone once said to me, "even the tiniest drop of food coloring can change the color of water." Since even our brief encounters can have a permeating effect on people, we should ground them in prayer to have the most positive impact.

In the book, *The Soul of the Apostolate*, author Dom Jean-Baptiste Chautard draws on an analogy from French monk St. Bernard about the importance of prayer in the souls of busy ministry workers; the advice, though, applies to all people of good will: he says we are to be reservoirs, not channels. With channels, water flows through, which is analogous to the busy soul who doesn't take time to pray and essentially runs on "empty," and ends up causing damage. In contrast, reservoirs fill up and the excess overflows—that is what we are to be like: filling up spiritually so that we can give what we have received.

Indeed we are told in John 15: 4-5: "Abide in me, and I in you. As the branch cannot bear fruit by itself, unless it abides in the vine, neither can you, unless you abide in me...apart from me you can do nothing."

Since only God sees the whole picture and knows the heart of the person, the more we call on Divine assistance, the better the person we're speaking with will be served.

I can testify to the importance of prayer and the danger that arises when we're lacking it. I distinctly recall a brief encounter with a student. I was tired, didn't take time to break and pray, and when he asked a question I was snappy in my response. He left in a huff and I thought sadly to myself, "I lost him." On other occasions, analogies and questions have come to mind seemingly out of nowhere, that have profoundly moved the hearts of the people I'm speaking with, and the difference was in those moments I had been drawing on the mind of Christ in prayer.

Let Love Be Your Aim

Author C.S. Lewis once wrote, "Love is not affectionate feeling, but a steady wish for the loved person's ultimate good as far as it can be obtained."[4]

I'll never forget the day one of my best friends came home from shopping. She excitedly told me about her new purchase, a jean skirt, and said she wanted my *honest* opinion. She told me she'd keep the tags on and if I didn't think it looked good she'd return it. She wanted to know what I really thought.

So she put it on and excitedly said, "Stephie, what do you think?! I want your *honest* opinion," she emphasized.

This was back in the day when dirty jeans were "in," back when brand new jeans looked like they'd been stained with mud and rust and then sold.

So I looked, and my opinion was that that style combined with the cut did not look good on her—in fact, it looked quite bad. I hesitated to tell her what I really thought, but I also knew she trusted my judgment—that's why she asked for it—and that she was really asking, "When people see this on me, do *you* think they will think it looks good or bad?" So I told her honestly I thought it was ugly and that she should return it. She did.

It may be a light-hearted example that we both laugh about now, but it proves the point: love is about wanting the other's good,[5] not about wanting the other to *feel* good. So if we truly care about people that means we will share truths with them that are *for their good,* even if those truths don't necessarily make one feel good.

Matthew Kelly makes that point well in his book *Perfectly Yourself: 9 Lessons for Enduring Happiness:*

> ...I have constantly asked myself: *What do I respect?* And at a deep level, I think there is only one thing I truly and deeply respect over and over again in time, and that is virtue. I respect virtue. Virtue inspires me. Virtue in other people challenges me. Virtue raises me up. Virtue allows me to catch a glimpse of what is possible. Virtue gives me hope for the future of humanity.

***

> Our culture has reduced all virtue to the universal virtue of niceness, which is no virtue at all. People comment, 'Oh, she is such a nice woman' or 'He is such a nice man,' which in essence very often means that this man or woman never says or does anything to upset the person making the comment, never ruffles any feathers, never challenges anyone to rise to greater virtue... I hope nobody who knows me ever describes me as 'nice' in this context. I hope to upset the people around me occasionally, to rattle them from time to time, to challenge them in ways that make them feel uneasy...

> Love makes demands upon us. To love someone means that from time to time you will be required by that love to tell someone something that they would rather not hear.[6]

Likewise, when sharing uncomfortable truths with people about abortion, we should remember those words. Of course, any way we can soften the hard things we have to say, we should. One way to do that is by narrating what you are about to do, saying things such as,

- "Because I care about you, I want to be honest with you…"
- "What I want to share with you is hard to say, but I believe you deserve to know…"
- "I want what's best for you, and if I don't tell you something I know, that you don't know, but would want to know, I would feel I've failed you as a friend…"

When imparting difficult truths it can be helpful to think of this analogy: imagine you wake up in a pitch-black dark room—so dark you cannot see your hand in front of your face. You start to move around but you bump into things. You don't know what's in the room as you don't know how you got there. What you need is some light.

Now imagine if all of a sudden the lights are flicked on. But these aren't ordinary lights—they are high-beam, movie-studio-quality spot lights. What would your first reaction be?

"Ouch! That hurts! Turn them off!"

All that time you wanted—needed—the light, but when you got it, you cried for it to go away. John 3:20 tells us, "For everyone who does evil hates the light, and does not come to the light, lest his deeds should be exposed." In a world where tens of millions of the youngest of our kind are killed through abortion annually, these are times of death and darkness. It is our job to bring forth a way of living that embraces life and light—but because that is so different from what our culture is currently used to, the "intensity" and "pain" of this light may cause some in the darkness to cry, "Go away!" Although people may seem to reject the light, they actually don't. What they reject is the *transition to* the light. It's not our job to avoid the transition—that can't be helped; it is our job to journey with them *through* the transition, knowing it is the loving thing to do.

Share, but Don't Dominate

In John 9:1-3 it says of Jesus that "[a]s he passed by, he saw a man blind from his birth. And his disciples asked him, 'Rabbi, who sinned, this man or his parents, that he was born blind?' Jesus answered, 'It was not that this man sinned, or his parents, but that the works of God might be made manifest in him.'"

When I was watching an interview of international speaker and author Nick Vujicic, a man born without arms and legs, I was struck by his reference to that passage as being particularly significant in his life. He understandably questioned God about "Why?" he was born lacking all four limbs. And when he read that passage of the Scriptures it all made sense: "that the works of God might be made manifest in him."

There is no denying that it is *because* Nick doesn't have limbs that he is so uniquely and beautifully positioned to inspire millions of people. He can give a message of hope and encouragement the way those lacking disabilities cannot. He meets with world leaders and gains access into places others wouldn't precisely because of what he *doesn't* have. His greatest obstacle has become his greatest opportunity. The fact that he has accomplished all he has, amidst his limbless state, is undoubtedly a testament to "the works of God [being] made manifest in him."

God uses our brokenness and His restoration to reach the

broken. And this applies not only to Nick, but to each of us. It's worth reflecting on our own challenges, whether physical, emotional, spiritual, psychological, or relational, and how we have, or are, working through these with God's grace. Then, we have an opportunity to be vulnerable to the people we have conversations with, people who often share with us their great challenges and burdens. We can share our own challenges and growth as they relate. Where someone may be experiencing despair, we can, through sharing our very life experiences, be a reason for hope.

Of course, when doing so we must be careful not to dominate the conversation with "our" stories, remembering that our focus must be outward—on the needs of the individual before us. We share to the extent it will help them, not to the extent it will help us.

Empathize

When training audiences about how to have fruitful conversations with the general public, I sometimes ask those in attendance to do the following exercise:

1. Think about a time when you did something wrong—and you realized that, whether in the moment or eventually. Think about when someone found out about it. What was their reaction? How did you feel in response to their reaction?

2. Think about one of your most embarrassing moments. What happened? How did others react? How did you feel in response to their reactions?

3. Think about a time you felt lonely—whether you had friends or not, you *felt* friendless. How did you feel and act during that time?

As people are comfortable, we share our experiences. Once, a person told a story of someone she confided in about wrongdoing, who got angry at her, and like a flower starting to bloom, she quickly closed up, afraid and ashamed. In contrast, another shared about a father-figure gently and compassionately hearing about her misdeed; she has returned to him on many occasions for wise counsel.

Then there were the embarrassing stories—one told a tale of a teacher whose face showed complete embarrassment that she looked like she would cry, but not wanting further embarrassment, she got angry at the student who was embarrassed too. Then there was the person who couldn't take a girl's embarrassment away, but she acted immediately and decisively to alleviate the embarrassment and protect the hurting friend.

Then there were the feelings of loneliness that led to wallowing in one's misery and isolating oneself further.

"Why do you think I had you do this exercise?" I'll ask the audience.

And I explain: when you speak with people about abortion, you will meet those who are embarrassed, ashamed, and lonely. Sometimes people appear angry, but as my friend Maaike has pointed out, it's often a mask for another emotion, like sadness or embarrassment. Maybe they'll start to realize their arguments are flawed. Maybe they'll have an epiphany about an abortion they were involved with. Maybe they're a lonely soul who doesn't have anyone to talk with. *Remember* those times you had similar feelings, *remember* the painful reactions of people around you who made it worse, and make sure you never, ever, treat anyone like that.

Then remember the times someone showed you compassion, grace, kindness, gentleness, and understanding when you had painful realizations, embarrassment, shame, or felt alone, and be that person to the souls you encounter.

Looks Matter

Have you ever seen a person look at another and sense that their gaze radiates total respect and kindness—as though there's a light switch behind their eyes and it's been turned on bright?

In another one of Nick Vujicic's interviews (yes, I'm a fan), this time on 60 Minutes Australia ("No Limbs, No Limits," August 3, 2008), he reflects this very powerfully. The interviewer makes the observation that people who preach and evangelize normally use their arms, but because Nick doesn't have those limbs, he asks about whether Nick instead reaches people with his eyes.

You can find that part of the interview online, and when you do, look closely at Nick's eyes.[7] They absolutely *radiate* peace, love, and compassion. Nick talks about the power of goodness from within being displayed through our eyes. And when people have conversations with us, a gaze like Nick's is the kind we want others to experience.

How does one achieve that? Prayer is certainly key. I remember one of my cousins telling me that before she went to her workplace she would pray, "Lord, help me serve…" and then she would list all the people she would encounter that day. Prayers like that, or reminding ourselves, "The person I am speaking with is made in God's image," or asking the Holy Spirit, "Please help me love her," will dispose us to giving caring glances.

Love Unleashes Life

One evening when I was chatting with a friend she remarked how one of her married friends said it is amazing, and beautiful, what happens to someone when they know they are loved. She cited her own spouse, saying her husband became this goofy, fun-loving guy who was comfortable in his skin once he was in relationship. Loving him let him be his true self.

When we are loved, we are like a flower coming into bloom — we are more fully alive. Something good gets unleashed; we know that who we are, as unique, unrepeatable selves, is valued.

When my friend shared that, I instantly thought of Maria*, the little girl my mom cared for in Romania when she and I travelled there in 2008 (that dream I mentioned in Chapter 1 that I fulfilled). Maria was 6 months old and weighed only 6 pounds. She had severe Fetal Alcohol Syndrome, other medical problems, and a large bed sore on her skeletal frame. She was sent to our clinic shortly before we arrived, and was placed in isolation—released for the first time when she was assigned to my mom.

When Maria sneezed you couldn't hear her. When she cried, which was rare, no sound came out. When you stroked her face to tickle her, she wouldn't even crack a smile.

She was flat. Emotionless. Unloved.

I presume all she had known from conception to then was neglect and abuse. She drew no attention to herself because no attention was ever given her. But then something changed.

Suddenly she was held. And rocked. And sung to. Suddenly she was kissed and cuddled. Her light—her life—was unleashed by my mom's love, and it was amazing what happened: she smiled, she laughed, and her cries made sound.

How many "Marias" will we encounter when we speak to people about abortion? How many have "checked out" of their lives because they have not experienced love?

Remember this: love unleashes life.

"I came that they may have life, and have it abundantly" (John 10:10).

Chapter 3
Communicating to the Head

With a solid foundation for communicating well, we're now ready to make an intellectual case against abortion. It's important to be well-equipped to respond to a broad range of objections abortion supporters may have. Whether we're speaking with someone who says the pre-born aren't human, or are not persons, or don't have a right to use a woman's body, we want to initiate such discussions with an open-ended question in order to decipher where a particular individual is coming from:

"What do *you* think about abortion?"

That question doesn't provoke the robotic "yes" or "no," but instead it compels thought—precisely what is needed in the abortion debate. With a majority of people supporting abortion in the first trimester of pregnancy (when a majority of abortions happen), it is vital that we invite critical thinking, and that question is a good way to start.

Although responses vary, there is a common theme. One generally hears, "I'm pro-choice," or, "I think it's necessary sometimes."

So we inquire, "When do you think it's necessary?"

And usually a litany of difficult circumstances follow: "Well, when a woman is raped. Or if she's poor. Or if she has no support. Or if she's really young. Or if the child is disabled."

And when those circumstances are brought up, they highlight something both those who support abortion and those who oppose abortion can agree on:

To be pregnant from rape would be difficult.
To be pregnant and poor would be difficult.
To be pregnant and have no support would be difficult.

So the pro-lifer can respond by saying, "I agree with you it would be extremely difficult to be pregnant and poor."

It is important to identify common ground[8] with those we are seeking to persuade. Finding common ground serves the important purposes of diffusing hostility, building a bridge of relationship with the person we are speaking with, showing that we have compassion, and helping the other person feel heard by us.

COMMON GROUND

When a person says something, ask yourself, "What do we agree on?" There's likely *something* you hold in common with them, and when you identify that, articulate it. Hearing, "I agree with you that..." or "If I'm hearing you right, it sounds like you're saying... and I agree with you there" is music to someone's ears. It can help diminish any tension the controversial topic is bringing up.

We see this in the Scriptures in Acts 17:22-23: "So Paul, standing in the middle of the Areopagus, said: 'Men of Athens, I perceive that in every way you are very religious. For as I passed along, and observed the objects of your worship, I found also an altar with this inscription: 'To an unknown god.' What therefore you worship as unknown, this I proclaim to you.'"

After identifying this common ground, the next goal is to try to move the person toward the pro-life position. One method to do that is to re-state their "difficult situation" in a different setting to show that they would not justify killing a born person in a situation similar to the one in which they advocated for abortion. We want to make the point that difficult circumstances facing one human do not justify homicide on other humans.

So we make an analogy, taking the circumstance given to justify abortion, and apply it to a similar circumstance but involving a born person instead[9]:

"Imagine a woman is not pregnant and poor; rather, imagine she's parenting a toddler and poor."

What we're doing here is a "test run" on whether that circumstance would justify killing a born child. We know it won't, and that will lead to establishing an important point. First, though, we end the analogy with this question:

"May she kill the toddler because she's poor?"

And what will the person say? "Of course not!"

So we follow up with another question: "If she may not kill the born child because of her poverty, then why may she kill the pre-born child because of her poverty?"

"That's different," they'll respond. "A toddler is a human being; a fetus isn't!"

The moment the abortion supporter responds that way (and many will), it shows we have drawn something very important out of them about their belief system:

1. They believe it is wrong to kill humans for reasons of poverty.
2. They do not believe the pre-born are humans.

The good news is we agree with them on the first point. What we have to do, then, is demonstrate the second point is a false belief.

These three steps of common ground, analogy, and question (taught well by my mentor Scott Klusendorf of Life Training Institute and Steve Wagner of Justice for All), can be applied to other difficult circumstances:

"What if a woman has no support; doesn't that justify abortion?"

Our response? Let's apply those steps:

1. **Common ground:** "I agree with you that to be pregnant and have no support would be really hard."
2. **Story/Analogy:** "Consider this: Imagine a woman had support until her child was five—*then* she suddenly lost all support."
3. **Question:** "May she kill her 5-year-old because she has no support in caring for him?"

"If no," we ask, "why, then, may she kill the pre-born child because she has no support?"

And yet again we may hear, "The pre-born isn't a child." And if so, that's what we need to figure out—and I will address how to respond to that assertion in the next section.

Perhaps the most commonly voiced objection is this: "What about rape?" I heard that sentiment on one of my frequent flights. The passenger next to me asked me what I did, so I explained that I educate people about abortion and asked him what he thought about abortion. He said, "I think it's needed, like in cases of rape."

I employed a response a friend of mine once suggested: "I agree with you that rape is horrible. Rapists should be thrown in jail and forced to do hard labor!" Sometimes after the common ground you can bypass the story/analogy and jump straight to a thought-provoking question, which I did in this case: "I have to ask myself, though, is it fair to give the death penalty to the innocent child?"

The guy became silent. He then said, "I never thought of it that way."

Let's dissect the strategy here: By starting off with what I agreed with him on, he felt heard. Moreover, by expressing what should happen to the rapist, I communicated how bad I think rape is—again, something he agrees with me on.

By focusing on the consequences for the rapist, I've set the stage for a powerful contrast to what he's proposing the consequences be for the child. It is here where language really matters. Pro-lifers *could* just say, "Is it fair to kill the child?" but that phrase doesn't have the same power as the question, "is it fair to give the ***death penalty*** to the ***innocent*** child?".

By using the terms "death penalty," I was indirectly contrasting the consequence facing a child conceived by rape (abortion, i.e., death penalty) with the consequence facing the rapist (i.e., no death penalty). By referring to the child as "innocent" I am, again, indirectly contrasting the child with the rapist (who, in contrast, is guilty). Regardless of debate over the legitimacy of the death penalty, **no one** thinks innocent people should face such a sentence.

Also notice that when I transitioned from common ground to a question, my phrase was lacking a word commonly used in interactions like this: but. Imagine after expressing outrage about rape I followed up with, "But is it fair...?" The use of the word "but" there would have sounded dismissive—like I didn't really mean what I said beforehand. That's not true, though: I did mean what I said, and I want the person to know that. So sometimes—but not all the time—it's best to leave "but" out.

What to use in place of "but" when connecting your common ground to a story or a question? Try these:

- "Imagine this..."
- "Consider this..."
- "I have to ask myself..."
- "What if..."

Human Rights

"Do you believe in human rights?"

That's a great question to ask someone we've conversed with as described above. Having asked countless numbers of people that question, I can confidently predict for you the response of people you ask that question of:

"Yes."

Once we get that affirmative answer, imagine we hold up

a fetal model, or a prenatal image, or an abortion victim photo, and ask, "What about *this* human's rights?"

That question is typically followed by this response:

"That's not human."

So we jump to another question that specifically addresses their claim about *what* the pre-born are (or are not according to them): "Are her parents human? In other words, is the pregnant woman human? Is her partner human? If yes, wouldn't it follow that their offspring must be human?"

Unable to counter that logic, the person will likely come back with this: "Even if it's human, it's not alive."

A Little Anecdote to Demonstrate the Power of Questions: I once dialogued with a university student who, when I asked what he thought about abortion, said he supported it. I asked a follow-up question and he declaratively said, "I have news for you—they're not alive." So I asked another question: "Then why would a woman have an abortion?" He paused, clearly not expecting that, and said, "Good point. Hold on, hold on, I have to go soon but I'll talk for a bit because it's rare to find someone who can think intelligently."

And so we ask a question that, this time, addresses the person's doubt about whether the pre-born could be living: "Well is she growing? Is the one-celled embryo growing into two cells, then four, and so forth? If yes, wouldn't it follow by virtue of her growth that she's alive?"

Language Matters: Notice how we're referring to the pre-born: as a she. She's not an "it" because born people aren't "its" and since the pre-born are equal to the born, we should be consistent in our use of language that references them. Of course, using "he" would be just as acceptable.

Those simple questions form the foundation of the pro-life case: that the pre-born are living human beings with human rights.

Our job is a bit like that of a trial lawyer. The lawyer's job is to compile evidence and present it in a compelling manner to convince a judge or jury of the validity of his claims. Making the pro-life case is, in a sense, like being in the court of public opinion and presenting information to draw people to the conclusion that an anti-abortion claim is the right one. Making an airtight case is key.

My friend Steve Wagner was asked by a car full of young women to explain his pro-life views at a stoplight late one night. He stammered, speechless in the face of the challenge. He decided that would never happen again, so he penned his "10-Second Pro-Life Apologist" and memorized it. Here's a variation on Steve's original[10] sound bite:

If something is growing, isn't it alive?
If someone has human parents, isn't she human?
And we humans have human rights, don't we?

If we have agreement on the initial premise—that humans have human rights—we simply need to convince our audience that pre-borns are 1) living and 2) humans. This aims the conversation on the main question pro-life leaders like Scott Klusendorf and Greg Koukl remind pro-lifers to focus on: What are the pre-born?[11]

Surprise! Significant Human Rights Doctrines Support an Anti-Abortion Position

When one reads widely acclaimed human rights documents and declarations, it becomes clear that according to these, pre-born humans should have the same basic protections as born humans.

For example, the *United Nations' Universal Declaration of Human Rights*[12] speaks of the value and right to life of everyone who claims membership in humanity and states that everyone should have legal personhood.

The UN also has a *Declaration of the Rights of the Child*[13] and it highlights that the lack of maturity and vulnerability of children means we should give them special protections, and it indicates this standard is not just for those who are born but also for those who are pre-born. It says children should be protected from being mistreated.

Then there is the *International Covenant on Civil and Political Rights*[14] which states that the death penalty cannot be given to a pregnant woman. This acknowledges that even *if* someone has committed a crime which some countries deem worthy of death, that innocent parties (such as pre-born children) must be protected from experiencing a consequence designed only for guilty parties.

The United States' *Declaration of Independence*[15] should also be viewed as a document that protects the pre-born because in highlighting that "all men are created equal" it speaks of the "unalienable [right to]...life."

Moreover, the *Canadian Charter of Rights and Freedoms*[16] expresses a similar sentiment and further expresses that one may not be discriminated against based on age.

As a result of these human rights doctrines we simply propose the following:

1. All human beings are entitled to human rights.
2. Pre-born children, of human parents, are human beings.
3. Therefore, pre-born children are entitled to human rights.

What Are the Pre-Born?

Once we lead the individual to the points that the pre-born must be alive because they're growing and must be human because their parents are, the individual is likely to object, "But it's just a fetus."

Time for another question: "What kind of fetus?" we ask.

"What do you mean?" the person may reply.

"Well," we respond, "the term fetus isn't species-specific. Dolphins have fetuses. Dogs have fetuses. And humans have fetuses. So what *kind* of fetus is she? What species does she belong to?" And logic will compel them to admit that it's the human species. It is here where we can frame abortion as age discrimination. Consider this dialogue:

"When someone gives birth, what do we refer to the child in their arms as?"

"A newborn," they'll say.

"Okay, and when that newborn turns two, what do we call her?"

"A toddler."

"Right. And what about when that toddler turns 13?"

"A teenager," they'll respond.

So then we summarize the point of asking those questions:

"So it seems that you and I agree that we humans have words to refer to different age-ranges in our species. The term fetus, or embryo, is like those other terms. They tell us *how old* someone is, but not *what* someone is. If we want to know what someone is, don't we ask, 'What are her parents?' And didn't you already acknowledge the parents are human?"

Usually the next objection goes something like this: "Okay, but you can't seriously think the one-celled embryo, the size of a speck, is equal to a pregnant woman, can you?"

So we ask, "Would you agree that you and I are humans equal to a pregnant woman?"

"Yes."

"And would you agree that the whole time we've existed—even when we were five—we were humans equal to a pregnant woman?"

"Sure."

"Okay, so why don't we start by figuring out when you and I began our lives? Would you agree there are only three options: Before fertilization, at fertilization, or sometime after fertilization?"

"Yeah, that makes sense."

"Okay, well let's consider each one to see which makes the most sense. Will the sperm in a man's body, by itself, ever develop into a young child?"

"No."

"Right. I agree with you. What about the eggs in a woman's body—will those, by themselves, ever grow into a young child?"

"No."

Cloning: It's possible when you ask about an egg, by itself, ever developing into a young child, people might say "yes, that could happen." But actually, it cannot. *Why* they may mistakenly believe otherwise is probably due to confusion about cloning. In that procedure, scientists take the 46 chromosomes of a cell, such as a skin cell, and place that into an egg that they have removed the DNA from. This requires human handling, and not even merely bringing together, but also directing electrical currents, or chemicals, to fuse the materials so they mimic what would happen in normal reproduction. But the egg cell itself (or skin cell for that matter) will not develop into a human.

"Right. Again, I agree. So it seems to me we could rule out the option of life beginning before fertilization.

"Yeah, I guess."

"Okay, now let's entertain the idea that life begins sometime *after* fertilization. If you encounter a young child walking down the road before you, would you ever think she fell from the sky and came to be that young child literally in that instant?"

"No, that's impossible."

"Agreed. If we saw a young child we would conclude she grew and matured from a younger version of herself, such as when she was an infant. But do infants appear out of nowhere? Is the stork story we may tell young children about birds delivering babies to doorsteps actually true?"

"Ha, of course not."

"Right. If we have an infant before us, we know she grew and matured from a younger version of herself, namely the fetal stage."

"Sure."

"So do late-term fetuses magically appear in women's wombs? Or do they grow and mature from a younger version of themselves, namely the embryo?"

"I guess the embryo."

"And doesn't the embryo come to be as a result of the sperm fertilizing the egg?"

"Yes."

"And whereas the sperm and egg—by themselves—only have half the genetic material that encompasses an individual, doesn't the one-celled embryo (also called a zygote) have *all* the genetic material that encompasses an individual?"

"I suppose. But so do my skin cells."

"Fair point. Let's consider for a moment—will a skin cell, by itself, placed in a uterus ever grow into a young child?"

"No."

"Correct. The skin cell may have genetic material but could be described as a human *part*, not a *whole* human. [17] But doesn't a one-celled embryo have what she needs within herself to move through the stages of human development? Yes, she needs food and the right environment to grow in, but don't you and I need food and the right environment to continue our growth too? Tiny as she is, isn't she a whole human?"

"I just don't see it."

"Do you mind if I explain with a story? It might help."

"Try me."

Those Who Claim They Don't Know When Life Begins Actually Do Know:

Isn't it interesting that when someone wants an abortion, they claim to not know when life begins, but when someone wants a baby, they know *precisely* when life begins?

Consider the reproductive technology industry (setting aside the ethics of such an industry, for the sake of this point): given they're in the business of creating life, they provide a great source to prove when life begins. After all, what moment do those creating life aim to replicate?

The moment of implantation?
The moment where the child feels pain?
The moment just before birth?

Reproductive technologists aim to replicate the moment of fertilization. They aren't satisfied with sperm and egg by themselves because they don't just want human parts; they want whole humans.

By their actions, these scientists communicate something to us that prevents the intellectually honest from maintaining the lie that "no one knows when life begins." They communicate that we *do* know when life begins; we know very well.

Or consider this: Have you ever heard veterinarians debate amongst themselves about when a dog's life begins? Do any of them say, "I just don't know when life begins for a dog"? Of course they don't say this—because when it comes to other species that reproduce sexually, we readily acknowledge that life begins at sperm-egg fusion, at fertilization. The fact that we claim to not know with our species what we absolutely know with others seems to convey that the problem is not that we don't know— it's that we don't *want* to know; because if life begins at fertilization, the implications for us are significant.

Moreover, here's more proof we actually do know life begins at fertilization: Consider the labels "3 months" or "6 months": these reveal the passage of time, and show that time is being "clocked" from a beginning point 3 or 6 months *prior.* So, if someone says life begins at 3 months, then they are actually implicitly acknowledging life began 3 months *ago.* If they say life begins at 6 months, then they are actually implicitly acknowledging life began 6 months ago, for that is the reason why they have marked the passage of 3 or 6 months' worth of time. So wherever abortion advocates draw a line, they are unwittingly making this major admission: that life began where they started clocking the passage of time that brought them to 3 or 6 months. So what happened 3 or 6 months prior? Fertilization. And that's when life begins.[18]

Starting Small—and In an Instant

At this point we can borrow a great analogy from law professor Richard Stith that involves Polaroid cameras and explains the difference between a developing thing and a constructed thing.[19] He makes a powerful point about something beginning in an instant by referencing a type of camera popular decades ago, in which a photo would print directly from a camera. I like to take Stith's point and make it personal by referencing my Scottish heritage:

"Are you familiar with the old photo technology called a Polaroid?"

"You mean those pictures you shake?"

"Exactly. You put a card in the camera. Snap, and when it comes out what do you see initially?"

"Black splotches."

"Right. So then you shake it and in a few minutes you see your developed photo, right?"

"Mhmm."

"Imagine you go on vacation to Scotland. And you decide to take your parents' trusty old Polaroid camera that you recently discovered they have. While in Scotland, you go on a boat tour of a famous lake called Loch Ness. Now what do people claim is in Loch Ness?"

"The monster."

"Right. So let's imagine while on this boat tour you take photos with the Polaroid camera. Mid-way through the tour, you look over your shoulder and suddenly see Nessie! You excitedly point your Polaroid in that direction and snap a photo. Just as the card comes out, Nessie goes under water. Will you be upset she's disappeared?"

"Kinda."

"What will make you less upset about her disappearance?"

"The photo."

"Right. Now let's imagine as you're shaking the card, a fellow tourist, who has never seen Polaroid technology, grabs the card from you to have a look. But instead of seeing Nessie, she sees the black splotches—and she incorrectly concludes the photo wasn't captured. With disappointment, she rips it and tosses it into the lake. Will you be upset?"

"Of course!"

"Me too. As you see her destroy the photo, you're probably envisioning all the money wash away that you could have made by selling the picture to newspapers and magazines. Now imagine, if in expressing your frustration to the tourist, she responds, 'But it was just black splotches. Why do black splotches matter to you?' And you'd likely reply, 'It wasn't just black splotches! Everything about the image of the Loch Ness Monster was captured *in an instant*! It just needed *time* to develop!' Couldn't we say the same about you and me? Who we are today was captured in the instant of fertilization, we just needed time to develop."

Embryology Texts Confirm that Life Begins at Fertilization: The pro-life website abort73.com provides a list of medical textbooks that clearly identify fertilization as the beginning of an individual's life. These include Keith L. Moore's book *Before We Are Born: Essentials of Embryology* and T. W. Sadler's book *Langman's Medical Embryology*.

You can view this list at abort73.com/abortion/medical_testimony/

"Fair enough, I see what you're saying, but even if the embryo is a human who begins to exist at fertilization, it's not a person."

Personhood

As with the use of the term "fetus," the word "person" needs to be defined. So we ask, "What is a person?"

If the individual we are speaking with has been influenced by Princeton philosophy professor Dr. Peter Singer, and others like him, she might say something like, "A person is someone who is conscious, rational, and self-aware."

Rather than argue about when in pregnancy the pre-born might become conscious, we address a more fundamental point: Human rights are grounded in *being* human, not in *behaving* human. But rather than push that claim in, we draw it out with questions. In this case, the "go to" question should be one that toddlers love to ask. And when they get their answer, they usually ask this same question again. And when they get their next answer, they once again appeal to the same question:

"Why?"

We ask, "Why isn't a human embryo conscious, rational, or self-aware?"

"Because it doesn't have a brain."

"Although brain waves have been detected at 6 weeks [learn more prenatal facts at www.ehd.org], certainly at fertilization the embryo doesn't have a brain. Could you tell me why she doesn't?"

"What do you mean?"

"Well what would be the reason for a one-celled embryo not having a brain?"

"It's obvious—it hasn't developed it yet."

"Fair enough. *Why* hasn't the embryo developed it yet?"

"It hasn't had the time."

"Right. I agree—the embryo can't ultimately think because she doesn't have a brain. And she doesn't have a brain because she hasn't developed a brain. And she hasn't developed a brain because she hasn't had the time yet. And time is reflected in our age. Why should our personhood be grounded in our age?"

"It's not. It's about being able to think."

"Okay, yet didn't you just tell me that she can't think because of how old she is? Why should those of us who are older have a right to kill those who are younger?"

"It's not about age."

"What is it about then?"

"The embryo isn't rational."

"Would you say a one-celled amoeba is also not rational?"

"Yes I would say that. And we don't give personhood status to amoebas!"

"Okay, and *why* would you say an amoeba is not rational?"

"It's not rational because it doesn't have a brain."

"Will it ever get a brain and be rational?"

"No, of course not."

"So would it be correct to say an amoeba isn't rational because of *what* it is? Namely, that it's not within its nature to be a rational creature?"

"Yes."

"I agree. And doesn't that answer tell us why amoebas aren't people but human embryos are?"

"Uh, I don't get how you got there."

"Well an amoeba isn't rational because of *what* it is. But as we already discussed, a human embryo isn't rational because of *how old* she is. One can't ever think. The other can't think *yet*—because of her age. A little earlier you said you believe in human rights, correct?"

"Yes."

"Who gets human rights?"

"Humans."

"Okay, well since we've established the pre-born are humans, then shouldn't they get the same human rights as you or me, regardless of their age?"

By bringing the discussion back to human rights, we are able to show that the legal, or philosophical, classification of "personhood" is ultimately irrelevant. But if they really push the issue of personhood, we frequently ask "why" in order to show that their definition of personhood would ultimately be grounded in age—which would be discriminatory.

After all, to define personhood based on a human's ethnicity would be wrong because ethnicity is something you cannot control, and isn't shared equally amongst all humans. Likewise, to define personhood based on age is discriminatory because it is something we cannot control, nor is it shared equally amongst all humans.

Or consider that in the earlier section about human rights doctrines, the UN Universal Declaration of Human rights indicates that everyone should get legal personhood status. This acknowledges that by simply having membership in humanity, one should get the legal protection of personhood.

When we make that point, however, the individual may bring up animal rights.

CONFUSING PERSON WITH PERSONALITY

Several years ago, a book called *The Vow* was released. It tells the true story of Kim & Krickitt Carpenter: Two months after their wedding, they were in a severe car accident. Krickitt was in a coma for weeks and when she woke up, she had no recollection of the previous year and a half of her life. It's been over two decades since that happened, and she has never been able to recall her memories from that time-frame—and that meant being unable to recall meeting, dating, and marrying her husband.

The story is meant to convey a powerful message about being faithful to one's vows in good times *and* in bad. When I was reflecting on the story, I thought about a philosophy professor I debated. This professor was very much focused on our identity being grounded in our brain and our thoughts and memories.

Krickitt is living proof that our minds can change and we can *feel* like a different person (upon coming out of her coma she had forgotten how to dress herself, brush her teeth, and walk) yet our identity remains the same. That doesn't mean our personalities will remain the same— these can change, as Krickitt, who struggled with angry outbursts afterwards, can attest to. Yet even when her personality changed, her person didn't. We can look at pictures of Krickitt now, of her in a coma, and of her pre-accident and we *know* that that is the same individual. Krickitt can look at pictures of herself, however, and have no recollection of some of those experiences; but her lack of remembering doesn't mean the experiences didn't exist, nor does it mean she didn't exist.

And so, as Scott Klusendorf taught me, the point is this: Here on this earth, thoughts and memories cannot exist without us, but we can exist without them—and that is as true for the pre-born as it is for Krickitt. We don't change what we are when we change what we know and remember. If we'd protect Krickitt pre-during-and-post coma regardless of whether she was thinking, then we need to protect the pre-born, too, regardless of whether they are thinking.

Animal Rights

"But aren't you discriminating against animals?"

"How does saying we believe in human rights result in discrimination against animals?"

"Well do animals get protections too?"

"Saying I believe we should make sure all humans are brought up to the level of how we treat most humans doesn't necessarily mean I disagree with bringing animals up to that same level. I'm not saying that I do or that I don't, which is an entirely separate issue. I'm just making this point: We could debate whether other species get protected like our species; can't we agree, though, that amongst our own species, we should all get equal protection?"

The point of directing the conversation this way is to avoid a debate about animal rights and keep the discussion centered on human rights. Alternatively, I sometimes respond with this:

"You know, your reference to animal rights reminds me of a Reader's Digest article from July 2012 which made the case for personhood for sperm whales because they exhibit higher-level behaviors we typically associate with persons."[20]

It may seem that we're creating a trap for ourselves because embryos can't do those things; however, we aren't. We continue: "But if we were to give personhood status to the sperm whale because of its impressive abilities, would we just give it to adult sperm whales or to all sperm whales, even pre-born ones?"

"All of them."

"Right; if we protect a species that has impressive abilities, we protect *all* within that species (including the pre-born whales), not just the adults. Wouldn't the same be true for humans?"

"I guess. But the fetus can't live without the mom. Doesn't that give women a right to abortion?"

Dependency

The individual is correct to note the total dependency of the pre-born on their mothers. Consider this: doesn't dependency of younger humans generally heighten the responsibility of older humans?

I was once debating abortion with a teenager who said, "Look, if you have a baby in one hand and a fetus in the other, you *obviously* pick the baby."

So I translated in my mind what she said. In other words, I thought about the two beings she was comparing—a born baby and a fetus—and I thought about how they were different. The baby is stronger; the fetus is weaker. So I thought to myself, "What she *really* said was something like this: 'If you have a strong person in one hand and a weak person in the other, you obviously pick the stronger!'" The moment I re-interpreted what she said I realized she didn't likely mean what she said.

And yet, it would have been futile to say to her, "I don't think you mean what you say," because she would have said, "I do too!" and I could have said, "Do not!" and round and round we'd go. Instead, I thought of questions and a story I could use to draw the belief out of her that we don't actually put stronger people ahead of weaker ones. Our exchange went something like this:

"You know," I responded, "What you just said reminds me of a picture a friend of mine posted on Facebook. It was a picture of a river, and in the middle of it there was something curve-shaped ever-so-slightly sticking out of the water. The caption with it said, 'My husband is a hero!' My friend went on to explain that at midnight, her husband, a paramedic, was called to the scene of an accident—a woman had been driving down the road, lost control of her vehicle, and it landed in a river. When my friend's husband arrived at the scene, the woman was sitting on the roof of her sinking car—with her 10-month old baby in her arms. The paramedic jumped into freezing water, swam to the car, and realized he could only take one person at a time to shore."

I ended with a question: "Who do you think he picked first?"

"The baby," she said.

"Right," I confirmed. "*Why* do you think he chose the baby first?"

"Well obviously," she declared, "If he picked the mom first the baby could have rolled in the river and drowned."

"Do you think he made the right choice?" I asked.

"Of course!" she said.

"So it seems to me that *you* believe that if someone is more needy, we help them first, not harm them," I said. "It sounds like you recognize that if someone needs more help, then we give them more help, not less. I bring that up because when you talk about a baby versus a fetus, you're really pointing out that the fetus is weaker, more vulnerable, and more dependent than the baby—and you're right. Based on your analysis of the paramedic's rescue, though, wouldn't that mean we put the fetus first, not hurt her?"

At the end of the conversation, the student said, "You argue well." Again, the power lies with questions and stories.

What is key in these encounters is that we draw on truths written on peoples' hearts. For example, most, if not all, in society would agree that our culture has advanced greatly in the realm of assisting the disabled. We have

- handicapped parking spots closer to the entrances of buildings
- elevators for those in wheelchairs
- ramps for those who cannot walk up stairs
- financial and social assistance programs to help those who struggle with physical and mental disabilities

What this reveals is that the more vulnerable someone is, the more a civil society recognizes the need to help them. Why does a person with a disability get to park closer to an entrance while I, who am more able-bodied, have to park farther away? Because I have what is needed to walk a great distance with ease, but someone with a disability may not. Why don't I get special treatment? Because I don't need it; the person with a disability does.

What does this tell us? The more someone needs help, the more we should help them—not harm them.

So the next time we speak with someone who says we need abortion for reasons of the dependency of the pre-born, whether because of their age or because of a disability, it is worth asking them to consider the ways our culture has advanced to help those who have a higher degree of dependency.

EVEN IF DIFFERENCES EXIST—DO THEY MATTER?

Author Stephen Schwarz, in his book *The Moral Question of Abortion*, coined the acronym SLED[21] as a way of remembering the four differences between the pre-born and the born that abortion supporters may use to justify abortion:

> **S**ize
> **L**evel of development
> **E**nvironment
> **D**ependency

The debate is not whether these differences exist—both abortion supporters and opponents can agree they do. The debate is this: do these differences matter when it comes to basic human rights? After all, these same differences exist between toddlers and teenagers, and we do not deprive toddlers of their right to life because of them—so why the pre-born?

Plus, these four differences ultimately boil down to age: the pre-born (or toddlers) are smaller than teenagers because in our species, at that age, that's the size we should be. The pre-born are less developed intellectually and physically because in our species, at that age, that's the developmental level we have. The pre-born are in their mothers' bodies because in our species, at that age, that's the environment we need. If we were elephants, we'd need our mothers' bodies for almost two years (I bet every woman reading this is feeling grateful she's not an elephant!). Finally, the pre-born are more dependent because, in our species, at that age, we require that kind of constant protection and nourishment.

Bodily Rights

With the case being easily made that the pre-born are human just like us, and that all the differences between them and us are ultimately irrelevant when it comes to human rights, abortion advocates sometimes take a different tact: they argue that the human right to life doesn't extend to a human right to use someone else's body to sustain one's life.

As a university student once said to me, "It's nice of me to donate my blood for someone else's body, but the law shouldn't force me to do that." A philosophy professor I once debated expressed a similar sentiment: It would be nice for a parent to donate her kidney to her ailing child but the law shouldn't force her.

Both of these are variations of an argument abortion supporter Judith Jarvis Thompson proposed in the 1970s about a famous violinist needing another's body to survive. What is the point each is trying to convey? It would be nice for a woman to "donate" her uterus to her pre-born child, but the law shouldn't force her. Their argument seems compelling—until we ask a question:

"What is the nature and purpose of the uterus versus the nature and purpose of the blood and kidneys?"

WHOSE BODY?

I once dialogued with a high school student who proposed a woman had a right to do what she wanted with her body. This is how our exchange ensued:

Me: "If I want to stand here and swing my arm, I have a right to do that, right?"

Teen: "Sure."

Me: "But what if I swing my arm to the point of hitting your friend in the face. Would you agree with me that would be wrong?

Teen: "Okay, yeah, okay."

Me: "So then it sounds like what you and I can agree on is that if I do something with my body that hurts someone else's body, you and I agree I shouldn't be allowed to do that. So the question is, is this the woman's body or the baby's body?"

The blood and kidneys exist in a person's body *for* that person's body. The uterus, however, is fundamentally different; as I explained when I addressed this point in Ethics & Medics (October 2009), the uterus exists in one person's body, every month getting ready for *someone else's body*.[22] Can a woman live without her uterus? Yes. Can an early pre-born child live without a woman's uterus? No. Those questions, and answers, tell us something: they tell us that the uterus exists *more* for one's offspring than for oneself. That doesn't mean the uterus doesn't serve beneficial purposes for a woman—it does; yet it still helps us see there's something different about the uterus, which is why whether we are obligated, or not, to share our blood or kidneys is a different matter entirely.

Further, someone with a medical condition who requires extra blood or kidneys is in a situation where something in the body has gone wrong. But someone in the first several months of her life who requires a uterus for a time is in a situation where something in the body has gone right.

Moreover, don't parents have a duty to ensure they meet the basic, or ordinary, needs of their children? For example, parents are not obligated to take their kids to Disneyland (although my eldest niece would wish otherwise), but they are obligated to feed, clothe, and shelter their children. Pregnancy is analogous to the latter, not the former. The uterus is what's needed to feed and shelter human offspring of a certain age, the way breasts or formula and cribs are needed for human offspring of other ages. Giving our kidneys or blood, however, would be extraordinary, like going to Disneyland.[23]

AIRPLANES AND WOMBS

One day, while on one of my many frequent flights, I began to ponder the parallels between pre-borns in pregnancy and individuals in airplanes. As my plane took off, I had an epiphany: this experience is as close as it gets to somewhat replicating the experience of a pre-born child. I am enclosed in a properly pressurized environment. I am powerless to control the plane. I am at the mercy of someone else.[24]

But in my case, I felt safe—and with good reason. Pilots are trained to get their passengers safely to the destination. It's hard to imagine, then, a pilot suddenly saying, "This is my airplane. I don't want you on it anymore; I've ordered the flight attendants to shoot you." Or, "I didn't know you got on the plane. I don't want you on it. I'm parachuting to safety and will let the plane crash with you on it."

Wouldn't we say such behavior is immoral? Wouldn't we echo the sentiment of Uncle Ben to Spiderman and speak of an interconnectedness between power and responsibility and say that where the former increases, so does the latter? Wouldn't we say that the pilot must use his power to fly the plane, and its passengers, to safety? Moreover, if pilots are expected to protect an adult who chose to get onto the plane, how much more should one protect a child who, without her knowledge, was placed somewhere (as is the case with the pre-born)?

The role and responsibilities of captains of major passenger vehicles—be it airplanes or otherwise—is something that has been highlighted in the news several times in recent years; it's also something I was able to parallel to abortion in a conversation with a student. I asked the student, Josh*, if he remembered the news story about the Costa Concordia, a cruise ship which struck a rock and started to sink off the coast of an Italian village in 2012. He knew exactly what I was referencing, so I asked him,

"This story made international news, not only because of the accident and because of people dying, but why? What element of the story shocked the world?"

He responded, "That the captain abandoned the ship."

"Right," I responded. "People were horrified that he got off before all the passengers did—before all the people dependent on him were safe. So, our world looked at his actions and said what—that they were right or wrong?"

"Wrong," he declared.

"Correct," I affirmed. "We reject what he did because he put himself before others. Now contrast his actions with those of another captain, but this time not of a cruise ship, but of an airplane: Three years before the Costa Concordia crash, another captain, Chesley Sullenberger ("Sully") faced a crisis. In his case, he was flying a US Airways flight when the engines were struck by a flock of Canadian geese. He managed to safely land his plane in New York's Hudson River. Then, as water was filling the cabin, he walked the aisle *twice* to make sure every passenger was off. He was the last person to leave the plane. What did our world say about him?" I asked.

"He's a hero!" The student said.

I responded, "And we look to his example as something to emulate because he put others *before* himself. Captain Sullenberger knew that having dependents made him *more* responsible, not less.

Upon reading Captain Sullenberger's autobiography[25], I discovered that he was following in the footsteps of a pilot like him who, decades earlier, was also forced by engine failure to make an emergency water landing— but this time, in the middle of the Pacific Ocean. Captain Richard Ogg also walked the aisle of his plane twice. All passengers and the pilot were saved before the plane sunk less than half an hour later.

We often ascribe the word "hero," as that student did, to people like Captains Ogg and Sullenberger. Though is that accurate? If we parallel their example to a woman faced with an unplanned pregnancy in order to encourage her to carry to term, we may hear what I did from an audience member: He said that I need to consider that not all women will think they can or want to live up to hero status. And furthermore, he wondered, from a public policy perspective, how can we create policy that forces people to be heroes?

So I asked him, "How would you define the term hero?"

And we discussed how heroes are generally individuals who go above and beyond the call of duty. And in that regard, even though we *think* of Sullenberger and Ogg as heroes, they are not, for they were simply doing their duty, as the requirements of a good captain are to meet the needs of their dependents, to put them first, and to use their skill and safety training for the benefit of all. So in that sense, a woman maintaining a pregnancy is not doing something "heroic" either in that she's not going above and beyond the call of duty; rather, she's meeting the ordinary needs required of her dependent (her child) and which are expected of her in her state of motherhood. And so, public policy opposing abortion is as legitimate as public policy demanding parents (or captains) fulfill their duty and meet the ordinary needs of their dependents.

Whether we use the term hero or not, those who are other-focused nonetheless provide a beautiful example for us to follow. Are they great people? Yes. Self-sacrificing? Absolutely. Virtuous? Indeed. They show us that with the power to control the destiny of others' lives comes the responsibility to protect and respect them.

Life in Danger

Because abortion directly and intentionally ends the life of an innocent human being, and because it is always wrong to directly and intentionally end the life of an innocent human being (such as a toddler), it would follow that abortion is never justified. So perhaps the most challenging case for even pro-lifers to face is the question, "What if a woman's life is in danger?" Many believe that this situation, at the very least, justifies abortion. Here is what I like to ask people:

"If we could save the mother's life without doing an abortion, do you think we should choose the non-abortion option?"

Almost everyone will agree "of course." Usually their affirmation is followed up with, "But sometimes you just *need* an abortion."

So then we can ask, "What medical condition in the *woman's body* will be fixed by us attacking the *baby's body*?"

Here again we see how language matters. The point of that question is to get people thinking that if the problem is a condition in the woman's body, then why are we focused on the child's body? Moreover, why would we *dismember* the child's body?

Having said that, some people may still resist, and although they often don't know the specifics of a medical condition to explain, they still hold their ground.

So then we impart this fundamental principle: "These are rare but tragic situations that warrant our attention and concern. When a woman's life is in danger, we should use the ethical remedies possible to save her life, and the good news is, with modern technology, we can do that. It is important to note that there are ways to address a woman's medical condition that do not involve directly and intentionally killing the innocent child; in other words, that don't involve abortion. So we do help the mom, we just don't kill the child. After all, consider this: If someone needed a heart transplant, would it be ethical to kidnap a stranger, have a black market doctor remove the stranger's heart, and place it in the other person?"

"Well no," they'll say.

"Why not?" we ask.

And they'll probably come up with some variation of this: "Because you can't kill someone just to save someone else."

And we find common ground: "Okay, and you know what? You and I can agree on that. It *is* wrong to kill one innocent person to save another; having said that, just because we may not kill doesn't mean there's no way to help. So if the woman's life is in danger, we're simply saying we can't kill the baby to save the mom, but there are other things we can do to help the mom. May I give you an example?"

Then we can explain the case of an ectopic pregnancy:

If a woman has an ectopic pregnancy where the baby is growing in the fallopian tube and we do nothing, her tube can burst, killing the baby and likely her. This is a serious medical problem that warrants our attention, concern, and intervention. There is a procedure called a salpingectomy, where the section of the fallopian tube that is expanding is removed. This will save the mother's life. Unfortunately, because we currently lack the technology to save the child, the little one will die.

In order to understand that this intervention is ethical, we can apply a concept called The Principle of Double Effect, which acknowledges that while we may not do wrong to bring about a good, when doing a good action to bring about a good effect, sometimes there is a bad effect too (hence "double" effect). There are various steps to this principle identified and bolded below (drawn from Edward Furton and Rev. Albert Moraczewski's essay *Double Effect*[26]).

The salpingectomy itself **is a good action** because it is removing a part of the mother's body that she doesn't need to live, that if left alone could result in her and the child's demise.

What is important is that we **do not do evil in order to bring about a good;** that is why abortion would be wrong: it would be doing evil in order to help the mom. In the case of salpingectomy, though, removing the tube, as mentioned above, is a good, not an evil, action. And the effect of the mother being saved flows, not from the bad effect of child dying, but rather from the good action itself of removing the tube.

Then there is **intention:** Those involved are not intending the bad effect of the child's death, but are merely tolerating it (if they could save the baby, they would). What they *are* intending is the good action and its good effect of the mother living.

Finally, when considering these effects, there must be **proportion** between them. In this case, the bad effect of the child dying is proportionate to the good effect of the mother living.

When people hear this, they often think that is no different from abortion, because the baby is dead whether with abortion or with a salpingectomy. So in order to show there is a significant difference, we want to ask questions to distinguish means from ends. Here is one way we can do that:

"Imagine two people write a test and get 100%. But one of them studied and the other one cheated. Would you agree that even though the end result is the same, that the means to get there are very different?"

Of course they'll agree. So we continue:

"Then it seems to me that you and I agree that we can't just look at the end result—we have to look at the means. So going back to this life-in-danger scenario, just because we have the same end of the child being dead, isn't it possible that the means are very different—and that one means could be very wrong?"

Or another analogy we can make to prove the point about means and ends is this:

"If two people are drowning and I jump in the water to rescue them but am only able to grab one and the other slips below the surface and drowns—have I killed the person who drowned?"

"Of course not," the individual will say.

We continue: "Correct. I was simply unable to save him. Now imagine when I jump in the water to save the one, I put my hand over the head of the other, and push him under water and he drowns. Have I now killed the other person?"

"Obviously, yeah," he'll reply.

So we conclude: "Right; I agree, and that shows us that even though the end result is the same in both cases (a person drowns), in one case I simply couldn't save the person, whereas in the other I directly killed him. So the principle is that simple if a woman's life is in danger: There are ethical ways to help the mom in which sometimes we can't save the baby, but that's not the same as directly killing the baby through abortion, which is always wrong. Does that sound reasonable to you?"

At the End of It All

There typically comes a point in the conversation where, if the person seems unconvinced, carrying on seems like it would be futile. I once spoke with a student for quite some time until we got to that point. So he used a common line:

"Let's agree to disagree."

And there was something jarring about that. The topic was too important to have such a careless attitude about, and yet it did seem pointless to keep the conversation going. So an idea popped to mind:

"Actually," I said, "Let's agree *that* we disagree. Let's agree that our disagreement is a problem. Let's agree that *if I'm wrong*, I'm spreading lies; if I'm wrong, I'm denying women's rights. However, let's agree that *if you're wrong*, you're permitting a grave injustice; *if you're wrong*, you're permitting the killing of people. So let's agree that we'll both continue to examine the issue and search for the truth. And truth, as Leo Tolstoy said, 'is obtained like gold, not by letting it grow bigger, but by washing off from it everything that isn't gold.'"

And that, he said, he could agree to. We smiled, shook hands, and parted ways.

When it's Actually Not the End

Sometimes conversations wrap up like mine did with the young man mentioned above. A good many other times they wrap up with people admitting to changing their minds, or at least to re-thinking their position. But there are still others who are closed—so closed that they aren't amiable and they certainly don't indicate movement on their opinion.

We may be too quick to conclude such individuals are closed-minded or hard-hearted. We may be tempted to quickly end the conversation because it doesn't appear to be going anywhere. And maybe it's not—because maybe, just maybe, we're asking the wrong questions.

It might be that the person is emotionally resisting the force of the logical argument because he is near changing his mind—and doesn't want to. So he needs something different than another dose of arguments.

From a logical perspective, there is no denying the power of the pro-life case articulated in this chapter. For people who are simply ignorant of the facts, the response should be that they readily change their minds. So if we're feeling like we're hitting our heads against a brick wall, then maybe we're not speaking with someone who's ignorant. Maybe we're speaking with someone who's in denial. If that's the case, it *will* be futile to continue to appeal to their heads when there is something going on in their hearts. Until we figure out what that "something" is, we're unlikely to get very far. That's why this next chapter is so vital.

Chapter 4

Communicating to the Heart

When I engage the culture through pro-life educational activity, people frequently reveal their pain to me. And in those moments I've realized the pro-lifer's task of being a voice for the pre-born also involves ministering compassion, love, and grace to the born. Moreover, I have seen that where people are coming from often influences their receptivity to our message.

For example, in just a few days of doing pro-life outreach, I and fellow team members met

- A student who had been raped the previous year
- A student who had been raped in the preceding weeks
- A student who had been hurt in the foster care system and whose closest relative had committed suicide the night before we met her
- A student with same sex attraction whose father, a pastor, sexually abused him
- A young woman who had an abortion at 15 and was now a single mom of a 2-year-old boy
- An abortion-rights activist whose own mother sold her for sex in order to obtain money to buy drugs

As Christian apologist Jojo Ruba points out,

"Logic can't help us explain to a hurting or confused student that they are a person of infinite worth. Neither science nor philosophy can change their minds. Only genuine love could touch them...though we should always have good reasons for the pro-life view, our main goal isn't to win arguments but it is to win people over."

Reaching hearts as well as minds means, as Jojo continues,

"being willing to stop just sharing facts and being willing to share our lives. In that way, these students can begin to understand that human life has great value because we treat them as people with great value. It's a good lesson to remember: that people need to know that when we say we are pro-life, we are also saying that we are pro-their lives."

What follows, then, is a series of conversations and insights I and others have had in which brokenness was brought to the forefront. The dialogues typically began on an intellectual level, but through true listening and keen observations, conversations were redirected to where they ultimately needed to go.

Lonely and Lifeless

While dialoguing with students at a pro-life exhibit on a university campus, one of my teammates applied the ideas of the previous chapter in conversation with a student named Pete*. After roughly 40 minutes of having no success convincing him to be pro-life, she asked Pete if she could introduce him to me, thinking that my experience put me in a better position to convince him that science and philosophy were on the pro-life side.

Important Lesson: If you identify the wrong problem, you'll come up with the wrong solution. What I was to discover was that Pete didn't need a more skilled or experienced debater. His problem wasn't a philosophical one. I was soon to see it was a personal one.

After introductions, Pete and I started debating. And after at least 30 minutes of going in circles about when biological life begins and how personhood is defined, I started to notice something about Pete's rhetoric—he repeatedly mentioned suffering, and was arguing that abortion was needed in such situations. It occurred to me I should ask a question that might just take us away from the head and into the heart:

Me: "Do you know anyone who's suffered a lot?"

❝ Do you know anyone..." When people focus like a laser beam on one circumstance when they believe abortion is necessary, it can be helpful to ask if they know anyone who's experienced that circumstance. This could draw to the surface their own life experiences, or their loved ones, but is less pointed and personal than asking, "Have you experienced..." which we would generally do well to avoid asking.

Pete: "Yeah, my mom and my siblings. We lived in poverty. We had nothing. My mom was beaten so badly by her husband that she ran away from him and lived on the streets for a time."

In that moment I had a revelation: Pete didn't want to kill humans. He cared for humans so much he didn't want them to suffer the way his mom and he had suffered. That didn't make his solution—abortion—the right one, but it did shed light on where he was coming from.

It reminds me of an experiment outlined in Dr. Robert Cialdini's book, *Influence: The Psychology of Persuasion*. The author tells of how three bowls of water, of three different temperatures: cold, room temperature, and hot, can be laid out in front of a person. Imagine an individual would place her left hand in the cold water and her right in the hot. Then she would remove both hands and together place them in the room temperature water.

What would it feel like?

To the left hand the room temperature water would *feel* hot, and to the right hand the room temperature water would *feel* cold. Actually, both would be "wrong" in that the water is room temperature, but the previous experience would color the present interpretation.[27]

So this is something for us to think about when it comes to circulating the pro-life message: What event/experience *precedes* the communication of our message? In Pete's case, it was great suffering. And that was influencing his response to abortion.

What merit was there in continuing on an intellectual discussion when it wouldn't ultimately address Pete's personal and painful experience?

Did I care for Pete as much as I care for pre-born children?

Was my encounter communicating that to Pete?

Would our exchange be an encouragement to him?

So I switched gears. I sought to understand. I expressed sympathy for his pain: "I'm sorry for your suffering," I said. I inquired about things currently: "How are you and your mom doing now?" And I encouraged him: "That's awesome you're at university!"

I decided to simply get to know Pete as a person. "What are you studying?" I asked.

"English," he said.

"That's great!" I responded. "I'm really passionate about good writing in this culture where it's quickly becoming a lost skill, so that's fantastic you are studying that!"

As I was listening to Pete, I wasn't just listening to his words. I was also listening to what was behind those words. I was "listening" to his mannerisms, his facial expressions, and his tone. And I noticed something.

Pete seemed down. Pete seemed lonely. Pete had an air of hopelessness about him. Could my female intuition have been off? Possibly. So there was one way to find out: ask questions.

"What do you want to do when you're done with school?" I asked.

"I don't know," said Pete dejectedly.

Trying to lighten the mood, and seeking an opportunity for comic relief, I said, "I hear ya. What do you do with an arts degree, eh? I have a BA myself."

Pete didn't have much of a response and unfortunately didn't crack a smile, but a new question popped into my mind, thanks to the Holy Spirit:

"Pete, what gives you joy?" I asked with a big smile on my face.

He paused, and then, with no emotion he slowly said, "Sitting in front of my TV and bringing a fistful of chips up to my mouth."

When I have shared that response with others, many initially responded with laughter. But when Pete answered me I had no inclination to laugh then, nor do I now. Because I don't think Pete was kidding. Sadness. Isolation. That's what I "heard" from Pete.

Trying to be hopeful, trying to believe it wasn't true, I smiled at him, and in a playful way said, "C'mon, Pete. When are you most fulfilled?"

And what he said broke my heart:

"When I'm sleeping."

I thought about my life and that of my family and friends and how, even amidst difficulties, we find so much fulfillment in relationships, in faith, in laughter, in helping others, in noticing the beauty around us, in enjoying the arts such as music or dance, or in the joy and comic-relief of children. But Pete didn't mention any of that. No, his moment of fulfillment was when he was completely cut off from it all, when he was unconscious.

It is so important to call on the Holy Spirit in crucial moments like these when a soul in need is in front of us. And so another question came to mind:

"Pete," I asked, "If you had access to unlimited resources to go *anywhere,* and do *anything,* what would you do?"

Phraseology Matters: Notice when I encouraged Pete to dream, I framed it in terms of "if you had access to *unlimited* resources." That was very important, because Pete had already conveyed his own financial hardship. So to simply ask him what he wants to do could be met with a dejected, "that's not possible." I intentionally framed the question so his present circumstances couldn't limit his dreams.

Suddenly, Pete's face lit up. He was silent for about 20 seconds as I watched something—I didn't yet know what— flash across his brain and cause his face to fill with delight.

"I'd go to Africa," he said. "I'd kill all the warlords. And I'd give everything back to the poor people that was taken from them."

Finally noticing animation and energy in his melancholy soul I said with joy and enthusiasm, "PETE! That's fantastic! I mean, I'm not so sure about the warlord part, but that's great you want to help people. Pete, you of all people know what it's like to suffer, and you want to help those who are suffering too. That's fantastic!"

"Oh," he said. "I know what you're going to do. You're going to ask me why I don't care for these people [pointing to images of aborted pre-born children] if I care about the others."

"Actually, Pete, I'm not," I said. "I sincerely am not going to make the connection. Pete, I want to abort the abortion conversation. Tell me more about your dream."

Pete was onto something—it *was* a perfect set-up to get back to abortion, but what would that have accomplished? My teammate and I had cumulatively already spent over an hour going through the arguments with him, and in deeply listening to Pete I realized he needed to be heard, to be encouraged, and to be given hope. That's what I was going to stay focused on. *I was deeply convicted Pete would not see the value in pre-born children unless he saw the value in himself.* And maybe thinking outside of the box would help get him there.

"Have you ever thought about going on a volunteer vacation?" I asked. I then told him about my dream to go to Eastern Europe and rock babies, and how I signed up for a volunteer vacation to do just that. I asked him to give me his e-mail and said I'd send him ideas for trips.

Language Matters: I didn't know whether Pete had a religious faith or background, so asking him if he'd thought about going on a "mission trip" could have been speaking a foreign language to him, and possibly even intimidating to him. But there are non-religious "volunteer vacations" that are much like a mission trip, and that's why I started with that.

I've had only one e-mail exchange with Pete since our meeting, and I don't know what he thinks about abortion now. I do know that when I sought to understand, and to get to know *him*, and to help him dream, that an otherwise sad soul lit up. I do know that this encounter reinforced in my mind the words my sister shared with me several years ago (penned by Bishop Untener of Saginaw, Michigan):

We plant the seeds that one day will grow. We water seeds already planted, knowing that they hold future promise. We lay foundations that will need further development. We provide yeast that produces far beyond our capabilities. We cannot do everything, and there is a sense of liberation in realizing that. This enables us to do something, and to do it very well. It may be incomplete, but it is a beginning, a step along the way, an opportunity for the Lord's grace to enter and do the rest. We may never see the end results, but that is the difference between the master builder and the worker. We are workers, not master builders; ministers, not messiahs.[28]

Hardship

More and more I hear from people that they believe suffering is legitimate grounds for abortion. I saw that, yet again, when speaking with a teenager, Mark*, who was defending abortion. He angrily said to me,

"What if you have a 12-year-old girl, raped by her father, pregnant with a deformed fetus, and she is going to die?"

Any one of those circumstances is a crisis in and of itself, let alone all in one experience. But as I listened to this student, I asked myself, "What is *behind* what he said? What is he *really* saying to me that perhaps he isn't verbalizing, but is what is underlying his words?"

So I re-phrased, in my mind, what he asked,

"What if you have a 12-year-old girl and her circumstances are hard, they're *hard*, they're *really, really* hard?"

Once I had identified what he *actually* said, I could more accurately address his concern.

"There's a lot there," I said. "And that's a fair question because those situations are reality for some people. I will give you an answer as you deserve; if you'll bear with me, part of me addressing your concerns involves asking you a question. It may seem off topic but I promise you it has a purpose: Is there anyone who inspires you?"

Why did I ask him that question? Because as I've been asking people that question for years (and its follow-up, "Why?") I have found it draws a fundamental principle out of them that people of all backgrounds can agree on. People typically have a different answer for "who" inspires them but a common reasoning for "why"; and it's that answer which will address what the student was *really* saying to me.

I have noticed that we humans tend to be inspired by people who suffer—who face obstacles, hardships, and difficulties. And what sets them apart from those who don't inspire is *how* they respond to their hardship: Inspiring people don't give up; they rise above. When they face an obstacle, they turn it into an opportunity. They are more focused on others than themselves. Inspiring people do the right thing, even when it's hard.

That was relevant because this teenager was promoting decision-making based on avoiding what's hard. My challenge was that I couldn't make the pro-life answer easy. I could make it eas*ier*, but I couldn't make it easy. Embracing my worldview would, in reality, be very, very hard. So how do I convince him to choose it anyway?

I tap into a belief he already has about doing the right thing even when it's difficult. I ask him who inspires him, and why, to draw out of him an example of someone who faced hardship but didn't give up, someone who did the right, but more difficult, thing. And then I ask him to follow in the footsteps of the person he admires.

Mark had an answer for me, but the person who inspired him was someone I knew nothing about. But that was okay—all I needed to know was to ask questions.

"I've never heard of him," I said. "Please tell me about him."

Mark proceeded to explain that he was a champion wrestler. "Did he have to work hard at his sport to succeed?" I asked.

"Oh yeah, for sure," he responded.

"So would there have been times when he was invited to certain fun things that he *wanted* to do but he would have said no to those because his deeper yes was to investing time in improving his skill?"

ʻʻThe only way to say no to anything is to have a deeper yes."[29] –Matthew Kelly

"Yeah," he said.

"And he excelled because of that, right?" I asked.

"Mhmm," he said.

I then asked more about this person, and Mark told me that the wrestler had faced a series of devastating tragedies, including the loss of relatives to suicide.

"That's awful," I said. "It perhaps was tempting to consider exiting from life himself in the face of such despair, but he didn't commit suicide himself, right?" I asked.

"No," he said, and we spoke about the inspiring man overcoming obstacles. As we went back and forth and I drew more and more out of him about the qualities of inspiring people; I then rounded it out by bringing it back to his original question:

"I asked you all that because when you brought up the difficult circumstances a pregnant 12-year-old could be in, what I really heard you saying is, 'What if someone is in a really hard and tragic situation?' And you just told me about someone who inspires you who faced hard and tragic situations in life. And you told me he inspired you, not because his life was free of difficulty (it wasn't), but precisely because of how he responded to all those difficulties. He didn't end a life, including his own, but instead sought to make something out of the life he had. He didn't give in or give up, but rose above. It wasn't easy, but he did the right thing. That's all I ask you to consider with crisis pregnancies—that we follow in the footsteps of inspiring people and not end a life, not give up, not give in, but look for ways to rise above and turn a tragedy into something good.

Mark got it. There was receptivity expressed all over his face. Whereas at the beginning of our conversation he had been resistant, suddenly he was pensive. He was contemplating all this, and his demeanor towards me had changed from hostility to kindness and warmth.

Author James Hunter, in his book *The World's Most Powerful Leadership Principle,* shares an important insight about how inspiring people don't have *easier lives* than us, but rather that they have *different perspectives* about their circumstances, and *that* changes everything:

> *One person goes to Vietnam, loses his arm and legs, returns home, and burns out on heroin. Another person goes to Vietnam and loses those same limbs, yet returns home and serves as the US senator from Georgia. Same stimulus, different response...This world between stimulus and response is the world of character. Character is our moral maturity and commitment to doing the right thing regardless of the personal costs.*[30]

Rape

After giving a lecture on a university campus, a female student got up during Q and A and asked about rape. I gave her my usual intellectual answer, as described in the previous chapter of this book, and she had a follow up question. Back and forth we went, with no receptivity on her end to the pro-life position that *how* someone was conceived doesn't give us license to end the life of *who* was conceived. Finally I said, "I have to move on and give other students a chance to ask questions, but I'm happy to speak one-on-one with you afterwards." Sure enough at the end she approached the podium for a private discussion.

We carried on where we left off, and my intuition kicked in: *Could she be a victim of sexual assault?* I wondered. *Or could she know someone who is?* We need to think in multiple dimensions. We have enduring pro-life principles, but there is more—those principles are applied to real people of different emotional make-ups, confronting real and difficult situations. Our tendency is to get caught up in the intellectual debate, when the real issue with many is not the principle, but some bad thing the person experienced, and their struggle to deal with it.

The pro-life position is logical, and if that's not getting through, maybe it's because her issue is actually an emotional one. I've met more than enough victims of sexual assault to notice that a person's singular focus on that reason for abortion is often indicative of a connection to that type of trauma. But how do I inquire without being too pointed on this most sensitive of subjects?

Life has taught me that sharing multiplies itself. I can remember opening up to one of my friends, sharing with her a vulnerable side of me, and when reflecting on why I picked that friend over others, I realized it was because she had previously confided in me, and her opening up gave me confidence to open up.

So I wondered if sharing was something that was needed with this audience member, too, and if doing so would draw the real issue out, leading us from the head to the heart.

"You know," I said to her, "I have a friend who was sexually assaulted; in fact, she was molested as a child. And in helping her get support, I've come to see whether someone gets pregnant from that or not, they've been traumatized, and an abortion isn't going to take the trauma of rape away."

"Yeah," she revealed with a deep understanding: "Ten years, and counting."

"I am so sorry," I said with sadness.

"I am sorry for your friend," she responded.

And in that moment everything changed. It wasn't about theories and arguments. We were talking about real people, and real pain. This knowledge didn't change what was objectively true, but it did change how I interacted with her.

Questions about her wellbeing, about how she was doing, and about whether she was getting help—these became first and foremost.

We parted very amicably, and there was something different, and positive, about the girl who departed from our private conversation versus when she'd asked her question from the crowd.

As my friends at Justice for All often point out, when people ask about rape, they typically aren't seeking to know if the baby is human; *they're seeking to know if the pro-lifer is human.* And so the words of civil rights leader Dr. Martin Luther King Jr., are very applicable here: *"Whom you would change you must first love, and they must know that you love them."*[31]

Sex-Selective Abortion

When something isn't getting through to someone's head, it's important we continually go back to the water experiment referenced earlier in the chapter and ask ourselves, "What was the temperature of the water their hand was originally in? Where are they coming from?"

That was the case for a physician who contacted me several years ago. She had a patient who was halfway through her pregnancy and had found out that she was carrying a female fetus; because of that, she wanted an abortion.

While many abortion supporters cringe at this reason for abortion, they still often defer to a relativistic response: "Well, if that's what the woman wants, who am I to stop her?" But this caring physician was unwilling to wash her hands of it all; instead, she sought to probe deeper, to find out "Why?" the patient wanted this.

She wrote to me that when she prayed about the situation, she had a strong urging to convey to the patient God's love for her.

And so, placing the patient and her husband as the last appointment of the day so she could give them as much of her time as needed, the doctor prepared to convey love. She sought to understand. And when she did, the patient opened up: She had an extremely traumatic childhood. She was abused—locked in a small room, deprived of the toilet, of food, and of water; at times she was even deprived of the warmth of a house and was instead shoved out into the cold. She was told her life was unnecessary because she was a girl.

Suddenly it all made sense: the woman didn't want to kill a girl. She wanted to spare a girl the suffering she herself had faced for being a girl. Because of her trauma it was understandable she felt that way, but it absolutely did not follow that her experience would be her daughter's. This was a tragic case where the problem was not the head—it was the heart, a heart which had experienced excruciating pain. Because the physician sought to understand *why* the woman wanted an abortion, because she listened and cared, the patient came to see that killing her baby girl wouldn't undo her own abuse.

Through all of this, the patient conveyed that she felt like her physician was the first person to try to understand her. Five months later, a baby girl was born. Her parents love her very much and are so happy they rejected abortion.

Personal Guilt

Or take the time I met a student named Trevor* while doing a pro-life exhibit. "What do you think about abortion?" I asked.

With hostility he told me that a woman had a "right to choose."

And so I asked questions; but as we respectfully dialogued back and forth for quite some time, it seemed we were going nowhere. Then suddenly he made an important disclosure:

"My girlfriend had an abortion eight years ago. It was the right decision and I don't regret it! I was a heroin and cocaine addict and I couldn't have raised a child."

Suddenly his hostility made perfect sense: he had a personal experience with abortion—one that he supported; that's why he was bothered by our presence and adamantly embraced abortion. At that point in our conversation I made a judgment call: He's seen abortion victim photography. I've conveyed the pro-life argument to him for the past 30 minutes. It's time to move from the head to the heart.

So we began to talk about his past drug addiction and he proudly declared he'd been clean for 6 years. I congratulated him.

"By the way," I said with a smile, "Here we are talking and I don't even know your name. I'm Stephanie."

And with a grin he shook my hand and introduced himself. His demeanor changed; he was warming up and our conversation continued, but less about "arguments" and more about life, his life.

I thought to myself that although he was adamantly expressing support for his girlfriend's abortion, it's possible if he doesn't secretly regret it now, that one day he may. And I wanted him to know that regardless of his past, he shouldn't despair; I wanted him to know there is hope. But how do you convey that to someone who is a self-proclaimed atheist? So I asked him a question:

"Have you ever done something you really regret?"

His initial response surprised me: "No," he said.

"Really?" I responded with shock. "There's nothing you regret? Wow, I regret things all the time. I'll think, 'Oh, Stephanie, what you did was really dumb,' or, 'You were really impatient with that person,' you know, mistakes."

"Well," he said, "Okay, there is something." And he made another striking disclosure: he'd actually only recently been "clean" for a year. He did heroin again the previous October after being clean for 5 years.

"Okay," I said, ensuring I avoided any tone of judgment, "And the next day, when you realized you shouldn't have done that, did you despair? Or did you tell yourself you couldn't change the past but you can improve and make a wiser decision next time?"

"Oh, the second option. I thought it was the stupidest thing I could have done and I was definitely not going to do it again," he responded. He explained that he knew he could still start fresh.

"Well," I responded, "I realize you don't regret the abortion, but I want you to know that *if* you ever do regret it, that you should never lose hope. You should hold the same attitude you do about the drugs you took, that you can't change the past, but you can make a different—a better—decision in the future."

We talked for a bit more and when he had to get to class I

said goodbye to a man whose whole demeanor had changed from agitation to peace and warmth.

As he was leaving I said, "By the way, I want to tell you again that I think it's fantastic you've been clean for a year, and you should be proud of that. Congratulations!"

And he smiled as anyone who's overcome a great obstacle should.

> ❝[W]e will so appeal to your heart and conscience that we will win you in the process." –Dr. Martin Luther King, Jr.[32]

With that, our encounter was no more. I don't know what he thinks now about abortion generally and about the abortion of his own child specifically, but I knew I could not make him feel something he did not feel.

What I could do, and what I did do, was draw out of him, from his own life experience, a memory of a time where he made a mistake and didn't despair. And I tapped into that—I asked him to remember that attitude and response so that if—*if*—at some future point he felt about the abortion what he felt about another bad choice he made, that he would respond with the same spirit of hope. I hope my showing of genuine concern for him will also move his thinking in the right direction on abortion.

On other occasions I have encountered women themselves who have had abortions. And many times what's needed in these situations is an expression of sympathy, a listening ear, and encouragement that will give hope.

One student I met who had been wounded in this way jumped into a conversation at a pro-life exhibit I was already having with three other female students—they weren't pro-life so I was explaining the pro-life position to them. This fourth female student, Emily*, echoed the sentiments they expressed and seemed agitated, but as I went through the logic of the pro-life perspective, the first three drifted away and it was just Emily and me, who started to "get" the logic and conceded it made sense if the science of when life begins was right.

But sometimes something that makes the most sense in our minds can be rejected because of what's going on in our hearts. And that's when she told me: "I was raped at 16 and had an abortion."

"I am so sorry," I said.

She told me that the rapist had been a relative. She got pregnant, and her mom drove her to an abortion clinic.

After we spoke about all this and how she was holding up, Emily changed topics and said, "I hear you guys have a baby with you."

Me: "Yes, we have a married couple on our team who brought their 3-month old baby Elizabeth with them."

Emily: "OH! That's so cool! [With great interest] Is she here right now?"

Me: "Yes. Would you like to see her?"

Emily: [With lots of excitement] "Really?! Could I?"

Me: "Sure, just come over to the back of the display with me."

Emily: [Shocked] "Really? Okay! For sure!"

As we walked, I was struck by her fascination and excitement about seeing a baby. I see them all the time; and hold them often—of course, I am delighted each time, but there was something out of place about Emily's response; it was as though she had never gotten close to a baby before. Maybe she didn't let herself, after the doctor ripped her own from her.

I picked up baby Elizabeth and brought her to Emily who smiled with joy upon seeing her.

"Do you want to hold her?" I asked. Again, Emily expressed both surprise and delight: "Could I?!"

And so I placed little Elizabeth in her arms and watched as this mother of a dead baby gently, lovingly, and peacefully embraced this living baby.

There seemed to be something healing, and hope-giving, about cradling a baby in her arms. Moreover, I was able to tell her about my friend Nicole Cooley[33] who wrote a book about how she was also raped, had an abortion, and regrets the choice she made (even saying it was more difficult to heal from the abortion than the rape).

Nicole once remarked,

"For years after my rape and abortion, I felt like I lived in a closed space densely filled with dust. Everything in my life felt muted and hazy. At the end of a stormy tunnel, I struggled to hear God's voice in my heart and could only do so with great straining and struggle-filled prayers. The oppression of my pain weighed me down physically, emotionally and spiritually. I could barely breathe. I felt broken, worthless, and depressed. Yet, through the fog, I could sense a faint ray of light and hope. Jesus loved me and extended His hand to me. Sometimes I took it. Sometimes I stubbornly refused His help and wallowed in my misery for awhile longer. Slowly, and often only out of sheer obedience to God by the strength of my love for Him, I began the climb out of my life's darkest pit. It is from the top of my rock that I am able to speak now. God is good. My victory is very sweet....I hope my story will encourage you to seek the healing and restoration available through faith in Jesus."[34]

When Emily left to go to class, she expressed that she had assumed the pro-lifers with the exhibit were going to yell and be mean, and how grateful she was that we were just the opposite to what she thought.

Indeed, kindness and mercy are most comforting in moments of conviction. Many years ago, a stranger, Beth*, called me after receiving a pamphlet that several friends and I had distributed at a pro-life demonstration. She sounded like she'd been crying, and confided in me that she had had three abortions and regretted them all. She was glad we had been witnessing with the pro-life message and although she mentioned she'd become a Christian, it sounded like she needed comfort. So I encouraged her to read Psalm 51 which says, in part,

"Have mercy on me, O God, according to thy steadfast love; according to thy abundant mercy blot out my transgressions. Wash me thoroughly from my iniquity, and cleanse me from my sin!...Create in me a clean heart, O God, and put a new and right spirit within me" (Psalm 51:1-2, 10).

Besides me mentioning this Psalm to her, Beth shared something with me: That she convinced two girls who were considering abortion to not go ahead with killing their babies. I was able to use that powerful story to remind her of this very important point: God can bring good out of the darkest places and mistakes we've made. He is a God of redemption. As we are reminded in Revelation 21:5, "Behold, I make all things new." Although we are powerless to undo the past, we do have, in the present moment, the power to do that which we wish we had done in the past. And it can be the regrets of the past that provide stronger motivation for behaving differently in the present. Beth was living proof of that, and it saved at least two lives!

Abuse

In another kind of encounter, I once met a student named Kevin* who resisted the idea that there is a scientific consensus that life begins at fertilization. I told him I'd be interested in seeing any evidence he has to back that up, but that my understanding was it is scientifically undisputed that life begins at fertilization. I began to explain the science and just as he was coming around to the facts and we were about to debate the notion of personhood, he had to get to class. But at the end of the day he returned and as we discussed the science and philosophy of the pro-life argument, viewing abortion as age-discrimination, he did a 180: "That makes sense," he said, "I can't argue with it. You're right."

I thanked him for his intellectual honesty and humility, at which point he said, "*But*, there are rare exceptions where if someone is going to be abused then abortion would be better."

That position didn't fit with what he had just admitted, and I began to wonder if his issue was one of the heart and not the head.

"Do you know someone who's been abused?" I asked.

"Yes," he said emphatically. "ME! My parents were crystal meth addicts. My father brutally abused me for six years. I was in and out of foster care, but was never able to be adopted because my mom refused to allow it."

"I am sorry," I said.

"No, no," he replied, "It has made me the stronger person I am today."

I responded, "When I said I'm sorry, what I meant was I'm sorry for the suffering you faced. No one should have to go through what you did. And while good can come from evil, it doesn't make the evil good. I don't doubt you have an amazingly strong character because of what you've endured, but what happened is still horrible."

He appreciated being heard but continued to justify abortion in those cases. So I asked if he wished he had been aborted.

"Now?" he said, "Now, I'm glad I'm alive. But there were times when the abuse was happening that I wished I was dead."

I conveyed that his feeling was completely understandable. Yet I was careful to ensure that while I validated feelings I didn't validate falsehoods. I then asked if he thought it would be better that we *alleviate suffering* instead of *eliminate sufferers*?

While there was some degree of receptivity to that point, he brought up the Holocaust and said there were some people who, in order to avoid the horrors of the Holocaust, may have killed themselves before the Nazis did. Wanting to distinguish between an understandable feeling and an objectively wrong action, I opted for a story. I asked if he'd ever heard of the book *Man's Search for Meaning* by Holocaust survivor Viktor Frankl.

He hadn't, so I explained that in Frankl's book he wrote about his arrival at a concentration camp and how he noticed some prisoners who, in the face of such torture and suffering, would kill themselves by running into the electric fence. Frankl decided early on he would never commit suicide. He wrote,

"...we had to teach the despairing men, that *it did not really matter what we expected from life, but rather what life expected from us.*"

He knew the suffering they faced was unjust, and should be stopped, but he also knew that the way to stop it was not with more killing. When he couldn't change the crisis he opted to change the perspective. In fact, Frankl also noted in his book,

"Everything can be taken from a man but one thing: the last of the human freedoms—to choose one's attitude in any given set of circumstances, to choose one's own way."

I then connected that back to a situation of abuse: don't we create a false dilemma by saying, "It's abuse or abortion"? Isn't there a third option? That we take all the energy and resources for abortion provision and instead put them into helping make sure children aren't abused? We can choose a better way.

"But," he objected, "You can't save everyone."

Does our inability to save all give us license to kill some?

Don't we become like the abusers when we do that—just switching one form of cruelty and torture for another, namely homicide?

And then a story came to mind. I recounted, as I best remembered, author Loren Eiseley's famous starfish tale:

I told him about a man was walking along a sandy shore which was littered with starfish; every few steps he would bend down, pick a starfish up, and toss it back to the ocean. Another man, observing this, approached and said, "What are you doing?"

The starfish thrower said, "I'm saving the starfish." The other man objected: "But you can't possibly help them all! This beach has starfish everywhere and you are just one man. You can't make a difference!"

The man bent down, picked up a starfish, tossed it in the ocean, and said, "I made a difference to that one."

Kevin looked at me with a smile on his face and with awe at my serendipitous story: "Funny you should reference that; it's my favorite story."

He told me his plan was to do social work, and help children in the very situation he had been in. I encouraged him in that, pointing out that he of all people was perfectly positioned to empathize and inspire such young people.

He left uplifted. He even gave me his address to which I mailed him a copy of Frankl's book. Do I know whether he abandoned his one "exception" for abortion? No, I don't, but I do know that I am one of many people Kevin will encounter in his life.

Scholar, teacher, and pastor, Cardinal John Henry Newman once prayed, "God has created me to do him some definite service; He has committed some work to me which he has not committed to another... I am a link in a chain, a bond of connection between persons."[35]

It is helpful to continually remember, "I am a link in a chain." While each of us needs to be a strong link, there are many links that are both before and after us.

> **"**I remember two cases of would-be suicide, which bore a striking similarity to each other. Both men had talked of their intentions to commit suicide. Both used the typical argument—they had nothing more to expect from life. In both cases it was a question of getting them to realize that life was still expecting something from them; something in the future was expected of them. We found, in fact, that for the one it was his child whom he adored and who was waiting for him in a foreign country. For the other it was a thing, not a person. This man was a scientist and had written a series of books which still needed to be finished. His work could not be done by anyone else, any more than another person could ever take the place of the father in his child's affections. This uniqueness and singleness which distinguishes each individual and gives a meaning to his existence has a bearing on creative work as much as it does on human love. When the impossibility of replacing a person is realized, it allows the responsibility which a man has for his existence and its continuance to appear in all its magnitude. A man who becomes conscious of the responsibility he bears toward a human being who affectionately waits for him, or to an unfinished work, will never be able to throw away his life."
> –Viktor Frankl

Poor Prenatal Diagnosis

It is an art, not a science, to truly reach those whose life experiences influence their receptivity to a message. That became clear to me when a student approached the microphone during a question and answer session I was doing at a university campus and said,

"My stepmom was told her baby was going to die at birth, so she had an abortion. Are you saying she was wrong?"

I thought to myself, how do I respond with charity and honesty? I began with an expression of sympathy:

"I'm sorry for your stepmom's suffering," I said. "That must have been a very difficult situation. Tragically in many situations like hers, the medical community too often fails patients by encouraging abortion."

Then I branched to addressing his point, and narrated to him what I was about to do: "Your question is a fair one and deserves an adequate response. If you'll bear with me, part of addressing your point involves asking you questions if you're willing to engage—is that okay?"

"Sure," he said.

"I'm going to use a thought experiment: I'd like you to imagine someone you love deeply and who lives on the opposite end of the country calls you today with horrible news: They've just been diagnosed with cancer and have been given four weeks left to live. Would you wait until week 3, day 6 to hop on a plane and say goodbye? Or would you get the first flight out and savor every moment of every day of the next four weeks with the person you love?"

"The second option," he said.

"Me too," I responded, finding common ground, and then I summarized the point:

"I think what both our responses show is that when we have a minimal amount of time left with someone we love, we maximize what minimal time we have left, rather than cut short the already short time, right?"

Then I bridged back to his original question:

"Now let's apply that principle to a poor prenatal diagnosis: A couple thought they had 50 years left with their child, but in one moment their world comes crashing down. If their child will die at birth, they realize they don't have 50 more years; they only have 20 more weeks. Why cut short the already short time with an abortion? Wouldn't we want to maximize the minimal time left? Wouldn't we want to savor every moment of every day of the next 20 weeks with the child we love?"

As I let that settle in, I thought about what was *behind* what he said, and thought that perhaps it was fear, fear of hardship and pain. So a good question I like to ask people is this:

"Why do you think abortion seems like the solution for people in that crisis?"

Inevitably people respond with something like this: "Because if they carry to term they'll experience the pain and sadness that comes with losing their child. They'll be asked throughout the rest of the pregnancy about the baby and it will make them feel sad that the continually discussed birth date will also be a death date."

"Fair enough," I reply. "Let's reflect on these questions: Will having an abortion take the sadness away? Will aborting the child abort the pain? The memories? Will having an abortion prevent the couple from being reminded every year on the expected due date or Christmas or other significant events, that they are missing a child?"

The point is this: The pain and hardship won't be taken away with an abortion. But the child will be. Memories and time that could have been cherished will be stolen by an abortion.

T.K. and Deidrea Laux realized this when they were faced with a poor prenatal diagnosis. Twenty weeks into their pregnancy, they found out their son, who they named Thomas, had Trisomy 13. They decided to carry through to term and Thomas lived for 5 days after birth. The Dallas Morning News followed them during their pregnancy and beyond, and in a 10-minute documentary featuring powerful reflections from this couple, Deidrea said,

"We knew it would be a hard road but I think sometimes when you make the toughest decisions you can get the greatest joy out of those. We didn't not terminate because we were hanging on to some sort of hope there was a medical mistake or there was going to be some sort of medical miracle. We didn't terminate because he's our son."[36]

PERINATAL HOSPICE

Dr. Byron Calhoun has developed perinatal hospice for families with children who are not likely to survive. He writes, "Families who choose to carry pregnancies in which a fetus has a lethal condition share many similarities with the families of a terminally ill adult or child member, clinical situations in which hospice has become an increasingly accepted and successful methodology of care. Many tenets of hospice can be applied directly to the circumstances of these families: an emphasis on neither hastening nor prolonging death; affirming life by caring for the loved one while regarding dying as a normal process; stressing values that go beyond the physical needs of the dying one; and meeting the medical, emotional, and spiritual needs of the family by providing a multidisciplinary team that continues to follow them even after the death of the loved one, during the period of bereavement....Hospice allows time—time for bonding, loving, and losing; time so that the entire course of living and dying is a gradual process that is not jarringly interrupted" (Hoeldtke NJ, Calhoun BC. "Perinatal hospice." American Journal of Obstetrics and Gynecology 2001;185:525-29).[37]

It was that attitude which carried them through the hard times, and enabled them to experience beauty amidst trial:

"I'm afraid to say goodbye," Deidrea said. "But I can't imagine what it would have been like to not have had this opportunity to go through this with him and to get to know him and to love him. It really has been amazing as opposed to just shoving it down and forgetting about it and pretending that his life didn't happen and that it didn't matter."

Deidrea's words show she knew that pretending that his life didn't happen wouldn't mean his life actually didn't happen. Her words show that suppression and denial ultimately don't help the grieving process. Moreover, she realized something that those who opt for abortion cannot say:

"The only thing Thomas will ever know in this world is love," said Deidrea.

Sometimes the prenatal diagnosis isn't about death at birth but instead is about a longer life with disabilities. All too often, less than "perfect" children are aborted. How do we change that?

As Frankl and many others teach us: it's all about perspective. In *Man's Search for Meaning*, Frankl tells of a severely depressed elderly man who sought his counsel:

> *He could not overcome the loss of his wife who had died two years before and whom he had loved above all else. Now how could I help him? What should I tell him? Well, I refrained from telling him anything, but instead confronted him with the question, 'What would have happened if you had died first, and your wife would have had to survive you?' 'Oh,' he said, 'for her this would have been terrible; how she would have suffered!' Whereupon I replied, 'You see, such a suffering has been spared her, and it is you who have spared her this suffering; but now, you have to pay for it by surviving and mourning her.' He said no word but shook my hand and calmly left my office. Suffering ceases to be suffering in some way at the moment it finds a meaning, such as the meaning of a sacrifice.*

Through this, Frankl teaches us the power of perspective — that we have the power to choose our response to circumstances we are powerless to choose. So it is with a poor prenatal diagnosis. The disability is beyond our control, but our response is not. Eliminating the poor attitude, rather than the child, should be our response. Emily Perl Kingsley helps us do that through her insightful reflection, "Welcome to Holland."[38]

She has the reader imagine planning for a trip to Italy, only to discover upon landing that after much preparation and anticipation, you weren't taken to Italy—you were taken to Holland instead. She explains that while initially it's natural to feel disappointed about all you'll miss out on about Italy, that we mustn't allow ourselves to stay in negative thinking. Instead, she encourages people to focus on the good things about the unexpected destination—all the beautiful, wonderful, and adventurous things Holland has to offer.

She likens this thought experiment to having a child with special needs—while it's natural to be disappointed that some dreams won't be fulfilled, one should focus on the goodness and joy that *can* be experienced from the unexpected situation. The essay beautifully points out that hardship and sadness won't go away entirely, yet there is a powerfully different, and beautiful, world that awaits someone faced with a poor prenatal diagnosis.

Photographer Rick Guidotti has made it his purpose to help capture this beauty in these different lives. His campaign is called "Positive Exposure" and he directs his vast experience of being a photographer for the fashion industry, into capturing the stunning beauty and powerful stories of those who live with differences, whether genetic, behavioral, or physical. One of Positive Exposure's exhibits is powerfully captioned, "Change how you see, see how you change."[39] It is perspective like that which is desperately needed in the abortion debate when it comes to facing a poor prenatal diagnosis.

A CHILD LIKE NO OTHER

A couple years ago I met author and speaker Leticia Velasquez, who wrote *A Special Mother is Born*, which includes her own story about raising a child with Down Syndrome. I was deeply struck by the portion where she talks about how, as her daughter Christina was sleeping in her arms, she thought about Jesus' mom mothering Him; she then meditated on the commonalities between Jesus and children with special needs. This was her inspiration:

> *Mary bore a Child like no other; A child who did not conform to society's expectations; He was different from the others; He gazed upon Heaven when the rest could only see clouds. He reminded them of their failings, their lack of charity, their shallowness, their impatience, and their rush to judgment. His government tried to kill Him, and eventually succeeded. He had to endure constant misunderstanding of what He was trying to communicate, and bore the frustration of those who misunderstood Him. He was mocked and rejected, and at times, it seemed only His mother still stood by Him.*
>
> *She felt the loneliness of seeing her Son rejected because He was different, yet she bore the pain patiently because she knew that it was for us, the 'least of these' that He suffered and died.*[40]

When Our Loved Ones Abort

I will never forget the conversation I had with Mike*. It was very philosophical. We were going around in circles about the definition of "person." Finally, I said, "Look, in my world you're safe. In my world, by being a member of the human family you are a person with a right to life. But in your world, you could be a victim of your own philosophy—someone else could come along, more powerful than you, with another arbitrary and discriminatory definition of 'person,' but one that has criteria that excludes you! But in my world, you have dignity, and value, and worth which cannot be annulled by a feature or ability. In my world, you're to be respected and protected simply for what you are—and no one can take that from you. In my world, you're safe."

And he looked at me with anger and pain in his eyes and he snapped, "In *your* world, I wouldn't exist!"

I had no idea what he meant. So I asked him,

"What do you mean?"

"My mom had an abortion!" he burst out. "She got pregnant with me just a few months after that abortion—if she'd never aborted my sibling she never would have conceived me."

It was as though scales suddenly dropped from my eyes. Everything Mike had been saying to me up to that moment was seen in a new light. And my heart broke for him. How does one wrap one's mind around the fact that his very existence—his very reason for being—is entirely tied up with the silent slaughter of his sibling? That has got to be devastatingly overwhelming to one's psyche.

Take all this, and throw into the mix the natural love and affection one has for his parents, now tainted by an instinctive disgust at the thought that those you love would do such a horrifying thing, and you have a perfect recipe for denial. For to admit the truth of the situation is far, far too painful for many.

I expressed my sorrow for Mike's loss and asked how his mom was doing and whether he thought of his sibling, but Mike didn't want to go there. I can only hope that our encounter in some way sowed seeds in his heart. Certainly he continued to wrestle with the issue because the following day he spent hours at a pro-life exhibit and spoke to several of my teammates.

I had a similar experience with another male student, Don*. Don and I were debating abortion and he was quite agitated, often cutting me off. Through our conversation I learned his sister had had an abortion. As his hostility wasn't going away, I began to wonder if he felt I judged his sister, if he felt that my position against abortion was somehow a personal attack against her.

So I asked him, "What do you think I think about your sister?"

I wanted to give him a chance to verbalize his thoughts, and often people are unwilling to do so until someone gives them permission. Interestingly, the moment I asked him that question, he softened: "Aw, you seem like a nice enough person; I know you probably wouldn't hate her."

I assured him that indeed I didn't hate his sister, and that I have friends who have had abortions. "How is your sister doing?" I asked. Later I inquired if he ever thought about his aborted niece or nephew and whether he thought about nicknaming the child and planting something in the child's honor as a way of memorializing the little one. Don's demeanor transformed before me when we stepped away from the intellectual arguments and talked about the real people in our real lives with real experiences and how people were doing.

Unfortunately I didn't see the same breakthrough with Melissa*, a student who wouldn't accept the science about life beginning at fertilization. Melissa disclosed that she was conceived by in-vitro fertilization (IVF). When I learned that, it made sense to me that she would have a hard time wrapping her mind around life beginning at fertilization — for the implications to her personally were grave.

Perhaps Melissa had longed for siblings her whole life, and if she admitted life begins at fertilization, then she would have to admit that she always did have siblings — but that they were kept frozen, or were experimented on, or were thawed to death. How many people had to be killed for Melissa to come to life? These are excruciatingly painful realizations — so painful that some default to denial. They prefer the conversation to be an intellectual one, but their own intellectual case is filled with holes and inconsistencies, because in making a defense of the mind, they're really trying to defend the heart.

Yet another young woman I met, Joanna*, was also conceived by IVF. Unlike Melissa, Joanna rejected the process for how she came to be. "My mom doesn't understand," she said to me. "She doesn't see how I can be against the very thing that made me exist." As Joanna acknowledged, she knows that she is a good result, and she very much values her life and wants to use her life to make the world a better place. She also knows that her mom had an understandable desire for children. It's just that Joanna acknowledges that good desires and good results don't add up to good means.

"I've seen the paperwork," Joanna said to me. "We were all just numbers." The cold and calculated filing system for handling human souls was something that touched Joanna deeply — she was one of those souls, and she knows that she is *not* a number.

Conversations about the beginning and ending of life affect

us deeply, because they touch us at the core of how we came to be. Why did I survive? Did someone lose his life so I could have mine? My loved ones are loving—they wouldn't hurt someone, or would they? Can I be forgiven for hurting the defenseless? These questions, and others, may not be verbalized to us in conversation. But they are often what is guiding people we have conversations with. So while we must have the strongest of minds, it is imperative we also have the most merciful of hearts.

QUESTIONS THAT APPEAL TO THE HEART:

- Do you know anyone who's experienced [insert: suffering, rape, abortion, etc.]?

- What gives you joy? When are you fulfilled? Why? I'm interested in knowing about that.

- Who inspires you? Why? What was their life like? Was it difficult? How did they respond to their challenges?

- Why do you think abortion will help?

- Have you ever done anything you really regret? When you realized that, how did you respond? Did you despair or instead seek to learn from your past to be better in the future?

- If someone you loved called you and said they were given four weeks left to live, would you wait until week 3 day 6 to visit them, or savor every moment of every day of the next four weeks with them?

- What do you think I think about your [sister, mom, friend, etc.]?

- Do you think your love for your [sister] is holding you back from opposing something she did? Do

- you think it's possible to love someone yet detest something they do? If your [sister, mother, etc.] drove drunk and killed someone, you would assumedly object to what she did, right? Yet wouldn't you still love her? Why not do the same regarding her abortion?"

- How is your [sister, mom, friend, etc.] doing?

- Do you ever think about your aborted [sibling, cousin, child, etc.]?

- Have you given yourself permission to grieve?

- Do you think someone has dignity regardless of how they were conceived? For example, whether someone was conceived by love, or a one-night stand, or an act of violence, that the individuals created are humans with human rights and human dignity? Wouldn't that follow for those conceived by IVF—that those individuals have human rights and human dignity as well?

- Do you mind if I ask, how old were you when you first learned about abortion? And what was your first opinion upon learning about it? Did you hold back then the view that you hold now? What changed? When did you embrace the view that you embrace now? [Note: One student I spoke with kept talking about when he was "15," so that told me something happened at 15. Further, children instinctively are pro-life, so if you encounter someone who learned about abortion at a young age and was pro-life but admits to becoming pro-abortion later, it's important to find out *what* happened to make them change their view.]

- I'm curious, where does your passion come from?

Conclusion

A friend of mine told me about a time he discussed abortion with a colleague that he worked with in construction. He shared the following:

"I was in the truck driving back from the job site with a co-worker when abortion came up. He asked me what the big deal was about abortion, so I began by asking him what he thought about it in light of what it was (the intentional killing of an innocent human being) and we went back and forth on some simple abortion facts. At one point (I was driving) I asked him to go into my wallet to retrieve some visual evidence of what abortion does to the child (I usually kept a couple of these 'business' cards on hand, along with a few cards for post-abortion help). The conversation was quite simple and went quite well, and by the end of about twenty minutes I could tell he was no longer on the fence.

"At the shop a few days later, a group of fellow workers were joking back and forth, and abortion came up. I was feeling pretty drained and wasn't really looking forward to defending the pro-life position, when all of a sudden the co-worker I had spoken to earlier in the week piped up 'Abortion?! That's totally wrong....' and started to articulate himself some of the same simple apologetic I had gone through with him earlier. I was really impressed and thankful hearing him champion what he had been hesitant to accept just a few days before."

Another friend of mine, an accountant, sent me an e-mail saying, "I spoke to a co-worker at work a couple of weeks ago who didn't really have any opinion on abortion. I used a couple of the arguments I learned from your talk. After I said about two sentences, my friend was immediately convinced and said 'Yeah! Abortion IS wrong.' I was so taken aback at how fast she made up her mind! And it made me think that a good chunk of people just really don't know too much about the subject and are open to learning about the truth."

My friend Devorah once spent some time with her friend Kelly* to teach Kelly how to talk with people who support abortion. Kelly then met with a friend, who was in favour of abortion, in a coffee shop and brought to the conversation a lot of what she'd learned from Devorah, and that friend changed her view.

Whether in a vehicle, in an office, or at a coffee shop, conversations about abortion are happening. We need more of these conversations, though, and that means people like *you* taking part. So please take my **7-Day, 3-Person Challenge**: In recent seminars I've given, I've asked audience members to put into practice what I taught them: "In the next week, I want you to approach three people and ask them what they think about abortion. For example, you could say to a friend, 'I went to this presentation about abortion the other evening and it occurred to me, you and I have never talked about the subject. What do you think about abortion?' Apply all you've learned, and then report back to me how the conversations go." You can submit your stories at www.stephaniegray.info.

Steven* recently took me up on the challenge, and on the seventh day (on the dot!) he sent me a summary of his conversations. Here's one of them:

> *This guy was pro-choice for sure. He talked about bodily autonomy. I countered this with your arm swinging analogy—how we can swing our arm but not if it hits someone because that's infringing on their rights...We went back and forth for a bit. I used the trot out the toddler*

argument. He then tried to question the humanity of the fetus. At this point, I could go down two paths. I knew that I could pull out the Keith Moore [see chapter 3] quote on the brochures or proceed with the three questions. I decided to go with the questions and have the Keith Moore quote at the ready as a backup. After all, you said it's better if they say it. It turns out I didn't need the Keith Moore quote. The questions were good. You were correct in saying that there is no particular order. This really got the point home. I was charitable throughout the whole discussion and he was pretty nervous by the end. I didn't want to embarrass him. I told him to think about what we talked about, then we'd meet again. He agreed. There is hope.

So please, use your reading of this book as impetus to start conversations in the next seven days, and ask three friends (or strangers!) what they think about abortion.

Employing the simple strategies of asking questions and telling stories, of reaching the mind as well as the heart, is having an impact:

For example, two teenagers spoke to my friend Cameron. At the beginning they thought abortion should be up to a woman, and even mentioned they had a pregnant friend who was abandoned by her boyfriend. As Cameron dialogued with them, they were transformed, saying they no longer supported abortion and were going to do everything they could to help their pregnant friend.

Or there's the woman who was forced by her mother to have an abortion at 14. Tears welled in her eyes as she spoke to my friend Lauren. The two of them formed a friendship and a few weeks later the woman said to Lauren: "Keep doing what you are doing. They say people like me should go out and get help—but we *need* people to come get us."

A teenager once told my friend Caroline that he was 50-50 on the abortion issue. After ten minutes of conversation he said, "This conversation made me do a complete 180. I no longer think abortion is acceptable."

A high school student told me that she used this information to discuss abortion with a classmate: "At the end of math class, although we didn't accomplish any math, [my friend] agreed that abortion was wrong no matter what."

The point of this book was to equip the average person to hold a meaningful conversation about abortion, whether they're moms chatting as they wait for kids after school, a nurse talking with a colleague on a break, a teacher dialoguing with a student, or anyone for that matter.

So if you've read this far, you are more than equipped. And if you think you can't remember it all, just remember to ask questions!

Appendix A

How to Communicate With a Friend Considering Abortion

"I'm pregnant, and I want an abortion."

How should one react when a friend says those words?

On various occasions I've been contacted by friends (and strangers) who have friends who are considering abortion. "What should I do?" they ask. "What should I say?" they wonder.

Their concern is the well-being of their friend and her pre-born child; they don't want her to go ahead with the abortion, but they come to pro-life educators because they recognize a noble desire, while necessary, is not sufficient to save a life. How do they actually *achieve* their mind-changing goal? They follow these four steps:

1. Seek to Understand
2. Support Her
3. Inform Her
4. Be Unwavering

Let's look at each in more detail, with practical tools to get the message out:

Seek to Understand

Think through your past to a time when you felt utterly overwhelmed and afraid. Think about an experience of despair where you felt helpless. Think about what it's like to feel panic — to feel trapped — and how that affects your decisions.

A woman facing an unplanned pregnancy may feel any number of emotions like the above, and anything you say or do is seen through the lens of what she's feeling. Rather than start your exchange by jumping onto a soap box, instead grab a Kleenex box, and ask questions that give her a chance to express herself.

Truly and deeply listen to her — what are her concerns? People not only need to be heard, they need to *feel* heard. This is achieved through affirming truth she's expressed, and communicating compassion:

- *"There is no denying that is a really difficult situation..."* or,
- *"That is really tough; I'm sorry for your suffering..."* or,
- *"This whole new reality must feel so overwhelming..."*

Notice what you're *not* doing here — you're not saying something false ("I know what it's like" when you, in fact, *don't* know what it's like); rather, you're formulating words that acknowledge you understand her feelings are consistent with her crisis.

From this expression of compassion, you seek to understand by asking questions that will give her a chance to express herself, and to help identify what she's most concerned about (which you need to know in order to address the problem — you cannot alleviate a problem you do not know exists).

For example, ask her, *"Why do you want an abortion?"*

Her response will likely involve expressing concerns about money, school, lack of support from her partner or family, feelings of inadequacy, or perhaps even pressure to abort.

What does this show? She does not desire abortion as an end in and of itself; rather, she sees it as a *means* to address a problem. Once she identifies the problem, suggest other means to address it, always through the approach of asking questions:

"I'm sad for you that your parents said they'd kick you out. You're right to be devastated by that. What if I was to let you live with me? Would that help? Or, What if I was to connect you to a place where you could live?"

"If I'm hearing you right, it sounds like you don't have the resources to care for a child. What if I was to connect you to a centre that will give you the resources you need?"

RESOURCES: Listing of pregnancy help centres:
- helpforpregnancy.ca
- heartbeatinternational.org

"It sounds like you don't feel prepared to parent a child right now, and I can understand that. What do you think about adoption?"

RESOURCES:
- adoptionincanada.ca
- theradiancefoundation
  (search "the beauty of adoption")
- bethany.org

"When a person receives a poor prenatal diagnosis, it can be scary to envision a future where the child has a disability. Have you

heard of stories of people who have had positive experiences caring for children with special needs? May I share some of these with you?"

RESOURCES:
- iamviable.com
- http://aspecialmotherisborn.blogspot.com/
- "Choosing Thomas" (search that title with "Dallas Morning News" on Youtube)

Questioning is not only important to identify her motivations to abort so you can provide alternatives, but questioning is an important tool to help her explore her "gut" feelings about abortion. Questions that help her think beyond the present scenario, to imagine a positive situation in the future when she's pregnant, can help bring to light her own negative feelings about the abortion procedure:

"Given that you just said you don't even love the child's father, I can understand it would be hard to envision parenting the baby. Something that's worth considering is if your scenario was just the opposite—if you were happily married and pregnant with a child you'd tried for so long to be pregnant with, would you ever consider abortion? [After her answer: *Why not?*]*"*

"If your parents wouldn't kick you out of the house, would you be less likely to consider abortion? Why?"

"If you had the financial resources you needed to raise another (or this) child, would you want to carry through with the pregnancy? Why do you think that is?"

The point of these questions is to draw out of her any instinctive feelings of revulsion toward abortion—if she articulates that she would never kill her child in these scenarios, you can now explore *her* thoughts that there is a child, and whether the difficulty of her situation changes what the child is.

Support Her

There's something terrifying about being alone in moments of crisis. There is something comforting about sharing, even a hard experience, with another soul.

A true friend will stand by her throughout this unplanned pregnancy. If she feels abandoned, then she may run to the abortion which she feels will get her "out" of this experience of crisis *and* "aloneness." Knowing she has someone to stand by her *through* the crisis will make it easier.

Offer to be with her when she has difficult conversations with her relatives or boyfriend/husband. Offer to go with her to the doctor. Time is of the essence in these situations and so is generous, selfless help. If you have to miss work or school to accompany her to a pro-life doctor the next morning, do it. Offer to accompany her to a pregnancy help centre. As a friend, it's important to remember you aren't a professional. Correspondingly, remember that professionals aren't friends, and offering to be present when she gets assistance from them will make her feel more supported than simply giving her a phone number to call.

When she gets professional assistance, ensure that the people you recommend are 100% pro-life. Tragically, some individuals and groups that are labeled "Christian" don't always hold a consistent pro-life ethic, and this requires you be extra vigilant in your recommendations.

Get to know your local pro-life doctors and local pregnancy care centre staff as soon as possible, *before* you meet someone in crisis. The more information you can give to your friend about who works where, what they offer, and how friendly they are, the more likely it will be that she will call or visit. And remember—offer to accompany her.

Part of being a support is helping her see goodness in a future that she thinks looks grim. Being on the outside, you have the chance to paint a picture of hope when she feels despair, to help her consider how short-term gain can bring about long-term pain, whereas short-term pain can bring about long-term gain.

This message, handed out by pro-life activist Mary Wagner to women going to abortion clinics, speaks important words of hope to women in crisis:

"You were made to love and to be loved. Your goodness is greater than the difficulties of your situation. Circumstances in life change. A new life, however tiny, brings the promise of unrepeatable joy. There is still hope!"

Inform Her

It is possible to communicate truth without love, but it is impossible to communicate love without truth. Loving your friend therefore means communicating the truth about the abortion she says she wants.

Certainly *how* you communicate that truth matters. You need to be sensitive and should continue to use questions as much as possible, but you nonetheless need to impart some hard truths. When providing information, you should convey three things:

- The humanity of her pre-born child,
- The inhumane nature of abortion, and
- How abortion can hurt her

Let's look at each of these in more detail:

The humanity of her pre-born child

A lot of women are unaware of just how rapidly their pre-born children are growing (for example, that a baby's heartbeat has been detected at 3 weeks, and brainwaves have been detected at 6 weeks—learn more prenatal facts at ehd.org). Ask a question like this:

"May I take you to a site which has amazing scientific facts of your baby's development?"

RESOURCE: ehd.org, a fetal-maternal health website with prenatal development facts, video footage, and 3D and 4D ultrasound

Helping her bond with her child is key; two other ways to do this is through giving her a fetal model to hold, which helps her visualize her baby, and encouraging her to give a nickname to her child, for it's harder to kill someone we've named and connected with.

RESOURCE: Order a first-trimester fetal model at lifecyclebooks.com (or ask your local pro-life society to give you one)

The inhumane nature of abortion

Remember, you're having this conversation with your friend because she said she wants an abortion. But does she know what abortion actually entails? It is essential that you convey the facts of the procedure. You can ask,

"What do you know of the abortion procedure? I have some knowledge of abortion and I believe you deserve to know what I do. May I share some information with you?"

RESOURCES:
- CCBR abortion videos: endthekilling.ca/videos
- Nucleus Medical Media: nucleusinc.com (search suction & curettage abortion at 9 weeks; D &E at 14 weeks).

When trying to explain that your motivation to share what you know comes from a place of goodness, you could use this analogy:

"Imagine there's water with poison in it—whoever drinks it will die. Now imagine you are thirsty and, not knowing the water is poisoned, you drink it. Would you have knowingly committed suicide?" She'll say no. Then continue, *"Now imagine that I know there's poison in the water and you don't. I see you grab the glass and I don't warn you what's in it. You drink it and die. Have I just been an accomplice to your murder?"* She'll say yes. Then connect the dots: *"In the same way, I know some pretty shocking things about the abortion procedure, and if I don't share these things, then I'd be guilty of withholding life-saving information. That's not fair to you."*

Some people have an unfounded fear that using abortion victim photography could do harm to a woman faced with an unplanned pregnancy. You don't lose anything by showing her pictures. But you potentially lose something by not showing the pictures: her baby's life.

Remember all the fears that are motivating your friend to abort? Those fears are very real in her mind; they are immediate problems. If she continues to maintain the idea that her pre-born child is not a baby and that abortion is not an act of violence that will kill that baby, then it will be easier for her to have the abortion than to deal with her problems. So while your challenge is to decrease her terror at the unplanned pregnancy by helping her solve her problems, it is also to make your friend more horrified of the abortion than she is terrified of her unplanned pregnancy. Abortion victim photography does that.

Admittedly, you need to be discerning in your one-on-one interactions about when to use any material. Be gentle, listen, and when it comes to showing pictures, tell her that you care for her and that you want her to be informed of everything she needs to know about abortion

Finally, be encouraged that using this information doesn't just work in theory—it works in practice. For example, a Los Angeles pregnancy center not only offers to show an abortion video to each client, but they provide a copy of that video for the client to take home. In 2011, they conducted a survey of all mothers who chose life for their babies at the centre after initially contemplating abortion. Eighty percent of their clients who chose life said the video was the number one thing that helped them choose life for their babies.

When the women take a copy of the video home with them, it also helps them to convince husbands, boyfriends, parents or other people who might be pressuring them to abort that abortion is a terrible choice. Showing the abortion video to parents pressuring their teen to abort helps them to understand the profound damage to their daughter (and grandchild) whom they love and want to protect. It is good to show the video to everyone influencing her decision. Further, some clients have reported giving their copy of the video to pregnant friends who in turn opted against abortion.

That is consistent with this post below one of the Canadian Centre for Bio-Ethical Reform's abortion videos on Youtube:

"A big thank you goes out to whoever posted this video. I scheduled an appointment with Planned Parenthood to have this

procedure and wanted to learn more because they wouldn't give me any information. I'm calling to cancel right now. I don't want my baby ripped to shreds."

How abortion can hurt her

Because abortion kills children it hurts women. It goes against human nature to kill one's offspring—that is why abortion can adversely affect women emotionally. It goes against the nature of a woman's body to unnaturally and prematurely interrupt pregnancy the way abortion does—that is why abortion can adversely affect women physically. Consider asking your friend,

"Have you heard about the complication risks of abortion? May I share what I know with you?"

RESOURCES:
- deveber.org
- abortionbreastcancer.com
- afterabortion.org
- silentnomoreawareness.org

Be Unwavering

Remember the earlier comment that being alone in moments of crisis is terrifying? That is true not only for the unplanned pregnancy, but also for the abortion procedure. The act of abortion could be, in her mind, a terrifying moment she wishes not to endure alone. Knowing she'll be without a friend could be enough to convince her not to do it. But if you are present, that could make her abortion experience easier to endure. This is why it is essential that if, after your best effort to convince her of abortion's wrongness, she goes ahead with the procedure, that you *not* go with her, *not* drop her off, *not* pick her up, *not* facilitate her decision in any way.

Keep this principle in mind: **friends don't drive friends to abortion clinics.** After all, if your friend was going to beat up her baby brother and you failed in convincing her not to, would you participate in that action, even if only to "be there to support her"?

If your friend does abort and then realizes at some future point that she made a mistake, and if you had in some way facilitated that abortion, she'll wonder why you did that when you knew it was wrong. She may even hold you partially responsible, and rightly so. But if you demonstrate integrity through your unwavering views and consistent action, this could be the factor that convinces your friend not to have the abortion—after all, actions speak louder than words.

Consider how you could explain your refusal to go with her:

"Because I love you, I can't go with you. Because to love you is to desire your good, and I know too much—I can't erase what I know about abortion and I know it won't be good for you or your baby. If I go with you, if I help you get there, then I'd be betraying you. I'd no longer be guided by what's best for you, but what's best for me (namely, just making sure you aren't mad at me). I love you enough that I'll endure you being mad at me—even feeling hate towards me—rather than help you do something I fear you'll regret in the future."

Hopefully, though, it won't come to making that statement. Because when you seek to understand and communicate truth in love, you can go far in convincing your friend to make a life-affirming choice. Then, you can journey with her, being present throughout her pregnancy and beyond.

Note: How to Communicate With a Friend Considering Abortion is available for purchase as a brochure from lifecyclebooks.com Item #668.

Acknowledgements

To the souls I have been privileged to meet and converse with over the years—thank you for opening your lives and teaching me how to listen and love better.

To the team, past and present, at the Canadian Centre for Bio-Ethical Reform who I had the joy of working alongside for twelve years to implement these principles with (in particular, Jojo Ruba, Brendan Huang, Steve Orlowski, Natalie Sanesh, Christine Tang, Michela Labonte, Hannah Carnes, Josh Nugent, Leah Hallman, Carlos Tolentino, Nicholas and Siobhan McLeod, Nick and Maaike Rosendal, Francisco and Alanna Gomez, Jonathon Van Maren, Devorah Gilman, Lauren Kyfiuk, Cameron and Catherine Cote, James and Ruth Shaw, Emil Booyink, Cameron Wilson, Erika Weber, Cristina Perri, Alex vande Bruinhorst, John Heikoop, Caroline Slingerland, McKenzie Schwittai, and Chandler Kerr, along with the many interns and anyone who I may have accidentally neglected to mention)—thank you for your self-sacrifice.

To my editors—Alex Philip, Alex vande Bruinhorst, Lauren Kyfiuk, Alanna Gomez, Julia Bright, Kathleen Dunn, Catherine Kilmer, James Borkowski, Jordan Lorence, Victoria Fausto, Devorah Gilman, Angela Christianson, and Margaret—thank you for your keen insights and helpful changes that have been invaluable contributions.

To Paul Broughton and the team at Life Cycle—thank you for accepting this manuscript and for working so hard to get it circulated far and wide.

To my pro-life mentors Scott Klusendorf, Gregg Cunningham, and John Hof who have been a constant source of information, formation, and encouragement for over a decade—thank you for carrying the torch high and lighting the way.

To the generous souls who have supported my full-time pro-life work, many of whom began doing so when I was that fresh-faced 21-year-old girl with a vision to make abortion unthinkable—thank you for your constant encouragement, prayers, and partnership; you have inspired me.

To my spiritual director Fr. T—thank you for your constant prayer, wisdom, and support, and for continually reminding me to "Seek ye first the kingdom of God, and His righteousness."

To my family—thank you for your unconditional love and support and for teaching me to never give up.

And most importantly, to my Heavenly Father—thank you for my life and your love. "Holy, holy, holy is the Lord God Almighty who was and is and is to come!...Worthy art thou, our Lord and God, to receive glory and honor and power, for thou didst create all things, and by thy will they existed and were created" (Revelation 4:8,11).

About the Author

Stephanie Gray is a seasoned and international speaker who began presenting at the age of 18. She has given over 800 pro-life presentations across North America as well as in the United Kingdom, Ireland, Austria, Latvia, Guatemala, and Costa Rica. She has spoken at many post-secondary institutions such as Yale University, George Washington University, the University of California, Berkeley, and the University of Sussex in England.

Stephanie has debated abortion advocates such as physicians who do abortions, which includes debating late-term abortionist Dr. Fraser Fellows in front of medical students at the University of Western Ontario's Schulich School of Medicine & Dentistry. She has also debated Ron Fitzsimmons, executive director of the National Coalition of Abortion Providers, Dr. Jan Narveson, Philosophy professor and recipient of the Order of Canada, and Elizabeth Cavendish, legal director for NARAL Pro-Choice America. Stephanie's audiences are vast, including medical students, churches of various denominations, seminaries, high schools, and pro-life organizations.

Stephanie has done hundreds of media interviews, which include being a guest on CTV News, CBC News, CBC's The Current, Global News, EWTN, Catholic Answers Radio, 100 Huntley Street's Listen Up, and the Miracle Channel's Insight. She has been interviewed by ABC-, NBC-, FOX-, and CBS-affiliated television news programs throughout the Midwest of the United States.

Much of Stephanie's media experience was generated during her 12 years as executive director and co-founder of the Canadian Centre for Bio-Ethical Reform, a ministry that took her to Alberta and Ontario. In 2014, she returned to her home province of British Columbia and now speaks on behalf of her ministry Love Unleashes Life.

Stephanie is Faculty at Blackstone Legal Fellowship where she trains law students from around the world about conversing persuasively on abortion. She is also author of A Physician's Guide to Discussing Abortion. Stephanie holds a Bachelor of Arts in Political Science from UBC in Vancouver, and a Certification, with Distinction, in Health Care Ethics, from the NCBC in Philadelphia.

Learn more at **www.stephaniegray.info**

Endnotes

1   He said this while teaching a pro-life apologetics training session in Florida in February 2012.

2   Over the years I've worked with many pro-life leaders who have emphasized the importance of employing the Socratic method of asking questions, as well as what I cover in a subsequent section: telling stories. In particular, Scott Klusendorf, Greg Koukl, and Steve Wagner have been shining examples of the importance of using these tactics.

3   Christian Renoux, "The Origin of the Peace Prayer of St. Francis," http://www.franciscan-archive.org/franciscana/peace.html, accessed September 16, 2015.

4   C.S. Lewis, "Answers to Questions on Christianity," *God in the Dock* (Michigan: Wm. B. Eerdmans Publishing Company, 2014), 37.

5   St. Thomas Aquinas (as cited in section 1766 of the Catechism of the Catholic Church, April 1995 edition) states this very beautifully as follows: "To love is to will the good of another."

6   Matthew Kelly, *Perfectly Yourself: 9 Lessons for Enduring Happiness* (New York: Ballantine Books, 2006), 63, 65.

7   "No Limbs, No Limits," *60 Minutes Australia,* August 3, 2008, http://sixtyminutes.ninemsn.com.au/stories/peteroverton/606750/no-limbs-no-limits, accessed September 16, 2015.

8   Stephen Wagner teaches this in his book *Common Ground Without Compromise* (California: Stand to Reason, 2008) and through his organization *Justice for All* and the apologetics training they teach.

9   Scott Klusendorf does this in his book *Pro-Life 101: A Step-by-Step Guide to Making Your Case Persuasively* (California, Stand to Reason Press, 2002) as does Gregory Koukl in his book *Precious Unborn Human Persons* (California, Stand to Reason Press, 1999).

10   Steve's original 3-step statement and his re-telling of the experience is titled "Got Ten Seconds?" and can be read online at http://jfaweb.org/Training/ADD/ADD_IG_TenSeconds.pdf.

11   As highlighted in Scott Klusendorf's book *Pro-Life 101: A Step-by-Step Guide to Making Your Case Persuasively* and Gregory Koukl's book *Precious Unborn Human Persons*.

12   This document can be read online here: http://www.un.org/en/documents/udhr/index.shtml. Pay particular attention to the preamble and articles 3, 6, and 7.

13   This declaration can be read here: http://www.unicef.org/malaysia/1959-Declaration-of-the-Rights-of-the-Child.pdf. Pay particular attention to the preamble as well as principles 1, 2, 5, 8, and 9.

14   This document can be read here: http://www.ohchr.org/en/professionalinterest/pages/ccpr.aspx. Article 6(5) references the death penalty.

15   This document can be read here: http://www.ushistory.org/declaration/document/index.htm.

16   This document can be read here: http://laws-lois.justice.gc.ca/eng/const/page-15.html. Pay particular attention to sections 7 and 15.

17   Robert George, along with Alfonso Gomez-Lobo, does an excellent job articulating the science of when life begins in their "Cloning Addendum" (2002) available here: http://www.inplainsite.org/html/cloning_addendum.html.

18   I made several of these points in a blog entry called "Do We Know When Life Begins" for Matt Fradd's website: http://mattfradd.com/do-we-know-when-life-begins/

19   Richard Stith, "Arguing with Pro-Choicers," *First Things*, November 2006, http://www.firstthings.com/web-exclusives/2006/11/stith-arguing-with-pro-choicer.

20   Jeff Warren, "Why Whales are People Too," *Reader's Digest*, July 2012, http://www.readersdigest.ca/magazine/true-stories/why-whales-are-people-too?page=0,0.

21   Stephen Schwarz, *The Moral Question of Abortion* (Chicago: Loyola University Press, 1990), 17.

22   Stephanie Gray, "A Kidney Versus the Uterus," *Ethics & Medics*, October 2009, vol 34, no 10.

23   This section drew from the article "A Kidney Versus the Uterus."

24   Ibid.

25   Chesley Sullenberger with Jeffrey Zaslow, *Highest Duty: My Search for What Really Matters"* (New York: HarperCollins Publishers, 2009), 44-45.

26   *Catholic Health Care Ethics: A Manual for Practitioners, 2nd ed*, edited by Edward J. Furton with Peter J. Cataldo and Albert S. Moraczewski, O.P. (Philadelphia: National Catholic Bioethics Center, 2009), 23-26.

27   Robert B. Cialdini, *Influence: The Psychology of Persuasion* (New York: Collins, 2007), 12.

28   Bishop Ken Untener, "Archbishop Oscar Romero Prayer: A Step Along the Way," http://www.usccb.org/prayer-and-worship/prayers-and-devotions/prayers/archbishop_romero_prayer.cfm, accessed September 16, 2015.

29   Matthew Kelly, *The Rhythm of Life: Living Every Day with Passion & Purpose* (New York: Fireside, 2005), 70.

30   James C. Hunter, *The World's Most Powerful Leadership Principles: How to Become a Servant Leader* (New York: Crown Business, 2004), 48-49.

31   Stated in a reflection by Fr. Richard John Neuhaus, "Telling the World Its Own Story," The Wilberforce Forum, July 2001, http://www.colsoncenter.org/search-library/search?view=searchdetail&id=21199, accessed September 16, 2015.

32   Al Kuettner, *March to a Promised Land: The Civil Rights Files of a White Reporter, 1952-1968* (Virginia: Capital Books, 2006), 61.

33   www.nicolewcooley.com

34   Nicole Cooley, "Questions and Answers about *Into the Light*," http://www.nicolewcooley.com/questions__answers, accessed September 16, 2015, "Help, I'm Hurting!" http://www.nicolewcooley.com/help_im_hurting, accessed September 16, 2015.

35   John Henry Newman, "Meditations on Christian Doctrine," http://www.newmanreader.org/works/meditations/meditations9.html, accessed September 16, 2015.

36   "Choosing Thomas," Dallas Morning News, http://www.dallasnews.com/sharedcontent/dws/photography/2009/thomas/.

37   Originally published in Stephanie Gray's booklet, *A Physician's Guide to Discussing Abortion, 2nd edition*, 20.

38   Available at http://www.our-kids.org/archives/Holland.html

39   Positive Exposure Exhibitions: http://positiveexposure.org/gallery/exhibitions/, accessed September 16, 2015.

40   Leticia Velasquez, *A Special Mother is Born* (Indiana: WestBow Press, 2011), xxii-xxiii.

SECOND EDITION

Daytrips
IRELAND

DISCARDED
From Nashville Public Library